*Encouragements
for the
Emotionally
Abused
WOMAN*

ALSO BY BEVERLY ENGEL:

Partners in Recovery
The Emotionally Abused Woman
Divorcing a Parent
The Right to Innocence

Encouragements for the Emotionally Abused WOMAN

Beverly Engel, M.F.C.C.

Fawcett Columbine • New York

A Fawcett Columbine Book
Published by Ballantine Books

Copyright © 1993 by RGA Publishing Group, Inc.

This edition published by arrangement with Lowell House.

Library of Congress Catalog Card Number: 93-90454

ISBN: 0-449-90878-X

Cover design by Judy Herbstman
Cover illustration by Judy Herbstman

Manufactured in the United States of America

First Ballantine Books Edition: March 1994

10 9 8 7 6 5 4 3 2

Table of Contents

Preface

- vii -

An Introduction to the Emotionally Abused Woman

- xi -

Are You Being Emotionally Abused?

- 1 -

Understanding Yourself—The Key to Change

- 27 -

Completing Unfinished Business

- 35 -

Should You Stay or Should You Leave?

- 61 -

If You Decide to Stay

- 85 -

If You Decide to Leave

- 101 -

Taking Time for Yourself

- 121 -

Raising Your Self-Esteem

- 155 -

Changing Your Pattern and Breaking the Cycle of Abuse

- 171 -

Continuing to Change

- 195 -

This book is dedicated to my mother, Olga Engel, who
died this year while I was working on it.
I know she would have appreciated it.

Preface

It has been two years since I wrote *The Emotionally Abused Woman*. Since that time I have received a great deal of feedback from women about how much they had needed the book and how much they appreciated my writing it. I already knew that the number of emotionally abused women was tremendous, and I was happy to discover that they had found my book and had benefited from it. But I also began to think that perhaps I could do more for these women in the way of offering support and reassurance.

Since it is extremely difficult to admit to being emotionally abused and even more difficult to leave an abusive relationship, women who have been emotionally abused need all the help they can get. I decided that a book offering reassurance and support for women who are currently being abused or who have recently escaped from an abusive relationship would be a much needed additional tool for their recovery. I didn't want to write a meditations book or an affirmations book exactly, but rather a book of encouragement, a companion book to *The Emotionally Abused Woman*—thus the title, *Encouragements for the Emotionally Abused Woman*.

If you are being emotionally abused, the abuser's insults, insinuations, criticism, and accusations slowly eat away at your self-esteem until you are incapable of judging the situation realistically. You become so beaten down emotionally that you blame yourself for the abuse.

For this reason, I wanted to write a book that would be an inspiration and a source of hope and wisdom. Unlike a meditations book with an entry for each day, *Encouragements* is organized around the recovery process itself, starting with the recognition that you are emotionally abused, continuing through the decision to leave the abusive relationship or to stay, and culminating in the growth you will need to experience in order to avoid abusive relationships in the future. Therefore, you can pick up the book and receive much-needed advice, encouragement, or inspiration during whatever stage of the recovery process you are in.

While people who emotionally abuse others don't always intend to destroy those around them, they do set out to control them. And what better way to control someone than to make her doubt her perceptions? What better way than to cause her to have such low self-esteem that she comes to believe she cannot survive on her own and that no one else would want her?

This is another reason why women who are being emotionally abused need constant reminding that they are indeed being abused, that it is not their fault, and that they can trust their perceptions. One of my main purposes is to provide an easy-to-read, accessible reminder that will help bring you back to reality, validate your perceptions of the situation, and offer you a way out.

If you have already read *The Emotionally Abused Woman*, these encouragements will inspire you to continue on your path to recovery from emotional abuse. If you have not read that book, you may wish to read it in conjunction with this one, for it will provide you with a great deal of information about emotional abuse and how to recover from it.

I have always had a deep respect for the wealth of wisdom that has been passed down to us in the form of quotations. From the time I was a little girl I remember writing down quotations that had an impact on me. When I was a teenager I started a notebook of quotations. I have long since lost that notebook, but my love for quotations has continued. It is uncanny how a simple statement can have a tremendous impact on us. A quote can soothe our pain, give us strength, touch the deepest parts of our soul, and even answer our most puzzling questions.

Choosing the quotes that I would use for this book was a very important part of the writing process. I wanted to offer quotes that would have special meaning to emotionally abused women, that would offer insight, strength, and wisdom particularly poignant to us.

My hope is that the quotes I have chosen, and the words I have been inspired to write because of them, will touch you the way they have touched me and that they will help to ease the pain, give you strength, provide you with hope, and sometimes even suggest a new way of thinking.

Each page of the book addresses a particular issue relevant to the recovery process. After each quote, a paragraph or two offers insights, feelings, or suggestions that relate to the subject. Sometimes the thoughts I share will be new information to you, other times they will be something you already know but perhaps need to be reminded of.

Each page concludes with an "encouragement"—a sentence or two that either sums up what has already been said on the page or introduces another aspect of the subject. The encouragements can be used as "thoughts for the day"; some, phrased in the first person, are particularly effective as affirmations.

Writing this book has been as much a gift to myself as anything I could wish to give to you. The quotations I found inspired me, nurtured me, and helped to bring me back to what is important in life—my emotional and physical well-being, my commitment to being the best person I can be, my need for solitude, and my communion with nature. As always, I learned some important lessons by writing this book, for the physician can never focus on herself and heal herself enough. As someone who was severely emotionally abused as a child I have spent my life recovering from its damage. Along the way, I have reenacted my abuse by surrounding myself with emotional abusers and by being emotionally abusive myself. Ironically, my own words helped to remind me of where I came from and where I wish to be going.

An Introduction to
the Emotionally Abused Woman

∽

Do You Recognize This Woman?

The emotionally abused woman was an emotionally abused child. While she may not recognize it, she has established an ongoing pattern of being abused by her lover or husband, her boss, her friends, her parents, her siblings, and even her own children. No matter how successful, how intelligent, or how attractive she is, she still feels "less than" other people. She may have taken assertiveness-training classes and yet still feels afraid to stand up for herself in her relationships. She is still victimized by her low self-esteem, her fear of authority figures, or her need to be taken care of by others. Although she has worked on herself through therapy, twelve-step programs, and/or self-help books, she often feels hopeless and increasingly critical of herself. She recognizes that despite her efforts to change, she seem to be unable to choose people who will treat her with respect and consideration.

If this sounds like a description of you, then you are an emotionally abused woman. Just what is emotional abuse? Emotional abuse can best be described as a process similar to brainwashing in that it systematically wears away at your self-confidence, sense of self-worth, trust in your perceptions, and self-concept. Whether this is accomplished by constant berating and belittling, by intimidation, or under the guise of so-called guidance or teaching, the results are similar. Eventually, you lose all sense of self and all remnants of personal value.

Many women suffer from the effects of emotional abuse—depression; lack of motivation; confusion; difficulty concentrating or making decisions; low self-esteem; feelings of failure, worthlessness, and hopelessness; self-blame; and self-destructiveness—but do not understand what is causing these symptoms. Often women will come into my office wondering what is wrong with them. They're depressed, they're not performing the way they want to at work and with their children, they've lost their sex drive, they're not taking care of themselves physically. As we talk, it becomes evident that someone in their life is emotionally abusing them.

Like many other women, you may not know that you are being emotionally abused. While you may realize that your husband, boyfriend, or boss seems to be demanding and hard to please, you may not consider his behavior abusive. Emotional abuse can be difficult to define. Unlike physical or sexual abuse, there is no physical evidence of the damage and there is no clear-cut definition of what is abusive and what is not. In addition, we all engage in emotionally abusive behavior from time to time, especially during arguments. So what exactly *is* emotionally abusive behavior?

The emotionally abusive person has an agenda, and that agenda is to be in control. He will therefore dominate, suppress, tyrannize, persecute, and attempt to conquer anyone he relates to on a consistent basis. Among his repertoire of control tactics are insults, denigrating comments, threats, and constant criticism, along with an extensive array of other intimidating behavior designed to make others feel inadequate and helpless. His most obvious tactics include yelling, threatening, temper tantrums, and name calling. These direct attacks have an aggressive, assaultive quality about them. But he also has an array of less obvious tactics that are insidious and covert, such as implied threats, unrelenting "constructive" criticism; gaslighting, denial, rewriting history, and shifting the blame.

You are being emotionally abused if:

- someone constantly criticizes you or feels his or her needs are more important than yours
- you wake up each day feeling worse about yourself than the day before
- you blame yourself for the problems in the relationship or situation even though you aren't quite sure what you've done wrong and even though you are trying as hard as you can
- your partner (or boss, or friend) always blames you for whatever goes wrong in his or her life

It is not uncommon for a woman to be emotionally abused by more than one person. The pattern of abuse often started when she was a child, so she has grown up with low self-esteem and the expectation of being abused. As a result, she continually attracts abusive people into her life.

Not all emotional abusers are male. Female bosses, teachers, friends, siblings, and lovers can be equally destructive to a woman's ego. In fact, some women use other, less assertive women as targets for acting out their anger and rage. Some women are misogynistic—that is, they have a deep dislike, distrust, and disdain for other women. And some women may be so envious of a female friend that they undermine and sabotage the friend's relationships or career.

Even though emotional abusers can be of either sex, most women reading this book will likely be concerned about their relationships with abusive boyfriends or husbands. Therefore, I will refer to the emotional abuser as "he" throughout unless I am specifically referring to a female abuser.

Encouragements
for the
Emotionally
Abused
WOMAN

Are You Being Emotionally Abused?

IT IS EXTREMELY DIFFICULT to come to the realization that you are being emotionally abused. To determine whether you are being emotionally abused, you need to work past any resistance you have to the idea, your continual doubting of yourself, and your tendency to give the abuser the benefit of the doubt. Even those women who already know they are being emotionally abused may go in and out of denial about how damaging the abuse really is.

The encouragements in the following section will help you determine whether you are indeed being emotionally abused and will help prevent you from slipping back into denial once you have admitted the abuse to yourself.

Admitting That You Are Being Emotionally Abused

∽

Look for a long time at what pleases you,
and longer still at what pains you.

COLETTE

It can be extremely difficult to admit to being emotionally abused, particularly if you feel competent and successful in all other respects. But emotional abuse is nothing to be ashamed of. And you certainly are not alone.

Admitting to this is going to require that you take a long, hard look at your relationships. How often are you in a state of emotional pain because of the expectations, comments, criticisms, or suggestions of those close to you? No matter how much you love these people, no matter how well-intentioned they may be, you do not deserve to be treated like a bad child. You are an adult who deserves respect, caring, and independence.

No matter how difficult and painful it is, admitting that you are being emotionally abused is the first step to recovery.

Doubting Yourself

*Doubt is a pain too lonely to know that
faith is his twin brother.*

KAHLIL GIBRAN

Because of the undermining nature of emotional abuse, because it rips away your self-esteem and causes you to doubt everything about yourself, you will most likely continue to question whether you are actually being emotionally abused.

This doubt is what the emotional abuser depends on. He knows you do not trust your own perceptions, knows that it is easy to confuse you. Don't let him get away with it! Begin to have some faith in your own feelings. If you believe you are being emotionally abused, then you are. It's that simple. Don't try to convince the abuser; he'll never admit it. Just keep trying to convince yourself.

Doubting yourself is like calling yourself a liar. Believe in yourself, trust yourself.

Cause and Effect

∽

We must never allow other people's
limited perceptions to define us.

VIRGINIA SATIR

Those who are being emotionally abused often come to believe their abusers' accusations. Emotionally abused women may become less and less productive, less motivated, less affectionate, and less sexual—but these are the *effects* of the emotional abuse, not its *cause*.

The next time the abuser tells you that the reason he is abusive is something you have done, remind yourself that no one is ever responsible for another person's actions. The next time the abuser tells you that he wouldn't get so angry with you if you would just try harder, remind yourself of how hard you have been trying and how little effect your efforts have had on his actions. And most important, the next time you are lying in bed crying over something the abuser has said or done, remind yourself of who you were before you met him.

I will not allow anyone—especially the abuser—to tell me who I am.

Self-Honesty

If one can actually revert to the truth, then a great deal of one's suffering can be erased—because a great deal of one's suffering is based on sheer lies.

R. D. LAING

Being honest with ourselves is probably the hardest kind of honesty. We lie to ourselves in so many ways: by minimizing the abuse and its effect on us, by making excuses for the abuser's behavior, by telling ourselves that things will get better, hoping that the abuser will change. But you must begin to tell yourself the truth—the whole truth, as they say—and admit that you are being abused, that the abuser is not likely to change without some kind of intervention, and that the only way to solve the problem may be to leave the situation.

The lies we tell ourselves cause us more suffering, not less. They keep us in a situation that is so unhealthy for us that it damages us every day.

The Benefit of the Doubt

Oh, life is a glorious cycle of song.
A medley of extemporanea;
And love is a thing that can never go wrong;
And I am Marie of Roumania.

DOROTHY PARKER

It is incredibly painful to come to the recognition that someone you love, whom you want desperately to believe loves you in return, could be abusing you. Because of the feelings you have for him, it is especially difficult to recognize that you may be emotionally abused by a husband or lover. When we love someone, we tend to make excuses for his behavior; we always want to give him the benefit of the doubt. This is especially true when the other person is good to us in other ways.

As painful as it is to admit that we are being abused, it is even more painful to come to the conclusion that the person we love is someone we cannot afford to be around.

You've given him the benefit of the doubt long enough. Now it's time to give yourself the benefit of the truth.

Feeling Sorry for Yourself

∞

Often things are *as bad as they seem.*

SHELDON KOPP
What Took You So Long?

You may sometimes think that you are just feeling sorry for yourself or that you are making a big deal out of nothing. But emotional abuse *is* a big deal. It is something serious.

People use the term "feeling sorry for yourself" as if it were a bad thing. But what is so bad about feeling sorry for yourself? All it means is that you are feeling sad or depressed, or that you regret your choices in life. Who doesn't feel these things from time to time?

Feeling sorry for yourself (meaning that you are feeling the ramifications of your situation) is normal and healthy. If you aren't going to feel bad for yourself, who is?

Feeling sorry for yourself is a way of caring for yourself. It is like picking yourself up and comforting yourself after a bad fall.

Don't let anyone tell you not to feel sorry for yourself. You have a right to, and it may help you to see the situation more realistically.

Equality

One of the things about equality is not that you be
treated equally to a man, but that you treat yourself
equally to the way you treat a man.

MARLO THOMAS

The first step toward being treated equally is for you to begin
to treat yourself as well as you treat other people. Women
who have been emotionally abused tend to feel "less than"
other people, no matter how successful, intelligent, or attractive they are. Because they feel inferior, they tend to grant
others the respect, time, and consideration they do not give
themselves.

You are equal to everyone else. No one is better or worse
than you are. You deserve to receive consideration, respect,
and kindness from yourself and from others.

I will work at treating myself as well as I treat others.

Domination

∽

Unable to get our own way, often we settle for trying to prevent other people from getting their way.

SHELDON KOPP
What Took You So Long?

When you allow yourself to be dominated by someone else, you begin to lose respect for yourself. You become silently enraged, both at the person who is dominating you and at yourself for allowing the domination. Someone else is in control of your life, just as assuredly as if you were a slave obeying orders. You are no longer the mistress of your own destiny.

But this can change. Even though it is understandable that, because of your abusive childhood, you may be afraid to stand up to your oppressors, that is exactly what you need to do. As a child you adapted to abuse in order to survive; now you don't need to. As a child you were never aware that you could make a difference in your own life, but now you can. Because you have been afraid of taking on the responsibility of living for yourself, you have given up your power to someone else. Now you must take back that power.

You have the right to your own ideas and opinions, to make your own decisions, and to have things go your way at times. Stand up for those rights.

Verbal Abuse

∽

Sticks and stones will break your bones
but words will never harm you.

PROVERB

What a falsity this childhood rhyme is. Words can hurt as much as stones, and the wounds go deeper. In fact, verbal abuse is extremely damaging to self-esteem and self-image. Just as physical violence assaults the body, verbal abuse assaults the mind and spirit, causing wounds that are extremely difficult to heal; wounds such as self-consciousness, insecurity, lack of motivation, and even self-hatred.

Verbal abuse is an assault on your mind. No one has the right to damage your body, mind, or soul.

Unreasonable Expectations

. . . those serpents! There's no pleasing them!

LEWIS CARROLL
Alice's Adventures in Wonderland

It is difficult enough, even in a healthy relationship, to meet another person's expectations and still remain true to yourself and meet your own needs. But when the expectations are unreasonable, you can never win. It is unreasonable for someone to expect that you will put everything aside in order to satisfy his every whim. It is unreasonable for someone to expect you to anticipate his needs unless he communicates them to you. And it is extremely unreasonable for someone to expect that you will put up with selfishness, constant demands, and ingratitude indefinitely.

When you are with someone who is never pleased, it is time to stop trying to please him.

Emotional Blackmail

∽

There is no terror, Cassius, in your threats,
For I am armed so strong in honesty
That they pass by me as the idle wind,
Which I respect not.

SHAKESPEARE
Julius Caesar

A person is manipulating you with emotional blackmail whenever he threatens to end the relationship if you don't do what he wants, or when he rejects you or distances himself from you until you give in to his demands. Giving you the silent treatment or telling you, "If you loved me . . ." are common forms of emotional blackmail.

We need to be able to give our love, time, and attention freely and willingly, not because we are afraid of rejection or abandonment. When you allow yourself to be blackmailed, you will always be at the mercy of a blackmailer who continually raises his demands; once someone realizes that you can be manipulated, he knows he's got you.

Try calling a blackmailer's bluff and you might be pleasantly surprised at how fast he backs down.

Unpredictable Responses

∞

A man's home may seem to be his castle on the outside;
inside it is more often his nursery.

CLARE BOOTH LUCE

Life is unpredictable enough without your being involved with someone who is unpredictable. Whenever someone in your life reacts very differently at different times to the same behavior on your part, tells you one thing one day and the opposite the next, or frequently changes his mind, you are being abused by unpredictable responses. You never know what to expect because the rules are always changing. It's like living with a human time bomb. No one deserves to live always waiting for the next explosion.

I have a right to some consistency, stability, and pre-dictability in my life.

Constant Criticism

∞

Blown about by every wind of criticism.

SAMUEL JOHNSON

Why is it that lovers and friends seem to think they have the right to constantly criticize you, or that they were put on this earth to judge you? Over time, their unrelenting fault-finding undermines any good feelings you have about yourself and your accomplishments. Eventually, if you stay in an emotionally abusive relationship like this, you will become convinced that nothing you do is worthwhile.

In allowing constant criticism, you silently invite the emotional abuser to destroy your self-confidence and self-worth, and simultaneously to rob you of any opportunity to grow and to change the things you want to change in yourself. Like a plant, you cannot thrive and grow while constantly being pelted with hailstones and being deprived of the nourishment of the sun.

You deserve a healthy, nourishing environment where you can thrive, not just survive.

Character Assassination

*Character builds slowly, but it can be torn down
with incredible swiftness.*

FAITH BALDWIN

Someone who humiliates, criticizes, or makes fun of you in
front of others, discounts your achievements, constantly
blows your mistakes out of proportion, talks openly about
your past failures, or tells lies about you—all in an attempt to
discredit you in the eyes of others—is guilty of character
assassination.

Our character is the foundation upon which we build our
reputation and our sense of who we are. We cannot afford to
allow anyone, no matter how much we care about him, to
destroy our personal reputation.

**Don't allow someone to destroy your good name; it took
you too long to build it.**

Gaslighting

There is nothing wrong with you. Anyone who says
something is wrong is wrong.

RENAIS JEANNE HILL

The term gaslight comes from the movie of the same name,
in which a husband uses a variety of insidious techniques to
make his wife doubt her perceptions, her memory, and her
very sanity. When someone deliberately and continually
denies that certain events occurred or denies that he said
something when you know he did, or when he insinuates
that you are exaggerating or lying when he knows you aren't,
he is playing a very malicious and dangerous game.

Once you allow someone to make you question your own
perceptions, memory, or sanity on a consistent basis, you
have given up a vital part of yourself. You put yourself at risk
of losing the very sanity you wish to hold onto.

**Trust your perceptions and believe in yourself and no one
will be able to make you doubt your perceptions or yourself.**

Constant Chaos

∽

*The Queen turned crimson with fury, and, after glaring
at her for a moment like a wild beast, began screaming,
"Off with her head! Off with—"*

LEWIS CARROLL
Alice's Adventures in Wonderland

One type of emotional abuse is characterized by continual
upheaval and discord. The abuser may deliberately start
arguments and habitually create conflict with you or others,
causing you to live in a tense, stressed-out, and off-balance
state. He may not intend to cause constant chaos, but he
may be addicted to drama. For many crisis-oriented people,
generating crises is the only way for them to feel alive.

You merit some harmony and peace in your life. You
probably grew up in a chaotic household and so you may be
used to living in the path of tornadoes, but it is not emotionally or physically healthy for you to do so. No one can
survive continual storms.

**You deserve some calmness and tranquility in your life.
You've already been through enough storms.**

Sexual Harassment

The Everlasting No.

THOMAS CARLYLE

Although this term is used most often with regard to work settings, a woman can be sexually harassed by anyone—a stranger on the street, a teacher, even a boyfriend or husband. Sexual harassment is defined as unwelcome sexual advances or physical or verbal conduct of a sexual nature. Whenever you are pressured into becoming sexual against your will, either because you don't choose that person as a sexual partner or because you don't feel like being sexual at the time, this is sexual harassment and you have a right to protest.

Sexual harassment is damaging not only because it objectifies women but because it carries the implied threat of rape. A remark that may seem harmless to a man can be a threat of violence to a woman.

You are not a sexual object and should not be treated like one.

The Emotional Abusers

*We first crush people to the earth, and then claim
the right of trampling on them forever,
because they are prostrate.*

LYDIA MARIA CHILD

Emotional abusers usually don't use physical force to trample
us. They don't have to. They have much more forceful
weapons to accomplish that end—words, attitudes, devastating looks of hatred, punishing silences. Instead of trampling
our bodies to the ground, they trample our minds, our hearts,
and our souls. Then, once we are defeated, empty, and half-
crazed from their onslaught of insults, innuendos, or
"advice," they turn to us and say, "What's wrong with you?
Get up off the floor, stop looking so pathetic, get some motivation!"

**Don't let the emotional abusers of the world trample you
to the ground. It's too hard to get up once you are down.**

Emotionally Abusive Mates
and Lovers

If you love me, you will suffer.

AGATHA CHRISTIE
Growing Up

Emotionally abusive lovers and mates can cause tremendous damage to our ego, to our soul, and mostly to our heart. Having won our trust, our vulnerability, our hearts, and our bodies, they have the power to absolutely devastate us.

Using a variety of tactics, an abusive husband or lover can damage your self-esteem, making you doubt your desirability and hate your body, causing you to feel as if no one else could ever possibly love or even like you. They can break your heart so badly that it will take years for it to mend, making it difficult if not impossible for you to trust anyone again.

No love is worth suffering for.

The Emotionally Abusive Mother

What the mother sings to the cradle
goes all the way down to the coffin.

HENRY WARD BEECHER

It has been said that a girl's mother is the most important person in her life. She is certainly the most influential. From her mother a girl learns to feel safety or to fear, to love herself or to hate herself, to value others or to take others for granted. From her mother she learns to be intimate or detached, possessive or freedom-giving. And from her mother she learns to be a mother herself. Most important, if a child's first intimate contact with another human being is emotionally abusive in nature, it will set the stage for all her future relationships.

Acknowledge how your mother has influenced you. Keep what works and begin to change the rest.

The Emotionally Abusive Father

∽

You stand at the blackboard, daddy,
In the picture I have of you.
A cleft in your chin instead of your foot
But no less a devil for that, no not
Any less the black man who
Bit my pretty red heart in two.

SYLVIA PLATH
"Daddy"

A girl's first perception of the opposite sex comes from her experience with her father. From this all-important relationship she develops her expectations of how a male should behave. As her first male love relationship, her father becomes her subconscious model for all future romantic encounters. It is vital that she feel her father's unconditional acceptance. If her father is emotionally abusive, she will in turn expect other important men in her life to be the same.

To develop self-assurance, a daughter needs to feel that her father accepts her and sees her as an attractive person both outside and inside. This acceptance provides the basis for her confidence as a woman and allows her to realize that she is worthwhile and that she should be respected in future relationships with men.

When a father gives his daughter the feeling that she is unattractive because he ignores her, criticizes her, or abandons her, he is paving the way for her to gravitate toward masochistic relationships in which she will be treated poorly.

Even though the magnet may be strong, it is possible to resist being attracted to abusive men like your father.

Emotionally Abusive Siblings

∽

When an older sibling establishes an abusive role with a younger sibling, the abuse often continues into adulthood unless one of them makes a concerted effort to change. The abuse may shift from physical to verbal attack or otherwise become more subtle and "grownup," but the feelings it evokes remain the same.

PATTI McDERMOTT
Sisters and Brothers

Unfortunately, all too often, a woman's sibling is her first emotional abuser. So-called sibling rivalry that begins in childhood often continues well into adulthood. While it is natural for siblings to compare themselves with one another and to feel competitive, sometimes what passes for sibling rivalry is actually emotional abuse.

In addition, sibling rivalry can cause us to develop a pattern of competing with our friends or being attracted to friends who always need to dominate us or compete with us.

It isn't until we discover who we are separate from our siblings, until we discover that we have our own unique qualities, regardless of who our siblings are, that we can break the chains of sibling rivalry.

Break the chains of sibling rivalry by learning to value your own unique qualities.

Emotionally Abusive Friends

*One is taught by experience to put a premium on those few
people who can appreciate you for what you are.*

GAIL GODWIN

Since we rely on our friends for honest feedback, support,
and companionship, they have a tremendous influence on
us. If they disapprove of our actions—our choices in partners, for example, or our job or career decisions—they can
influence our feelings about these things. Even if we disagree
with a friend's opinion, we usually assume that she has our
best interests at heart. But what if she doesn't? What if she is
operating out of envy, jealousy, or even out of a need to
destroy us?

There's a difference between a friend having an *opinion*
about something we are doing and having a *judgment* about
it. Opinions are merely points of view, judgments are indict-
ments against us or our actions.

**A true friend accepts us the way we are and states her
opinions without judging us. She has a strong enough
sense of self and enough love for us to not sabotage our
successes.**

Emotionally Abusive Bosses

Every woman adores a Fascist,
The boot in the face, the brute
Brute heart of a brute like you.

SYLVIA PLATH
"Daddy"

Bosses and other authority figures can make or break a woman's career and her very livelihood. Because of this, we tend to put up with behavior in work situations that we otherwise would not tolerate. Even the most assertive of women will be reluctant to confront a boss about his or her abusive behavior when it may mean risking her security or her children's security. However, if you can't confront an abusive boss and you can't leave an abusive work situation, you may end up paying a higher price than the loss of security—the price of damaged self-esteem.

No job is worth damaging your self-esteem for.

Emotionally Abusive Coworkers

∽

*When a woman behaves like a man, why doesn't she
behave like a nice man?*

EDITH EVANS

Even though our coworkers should be our allies, often they
become our enemies. Women may be emotionally abused by
male coworkers as well as female colleagues, but research
indicates that women are more likely to behave unethically
to other women than they are to men. Women tend to
engage in behind-the-scenes gossip, backstabbing, even con-
niving actions to achieve their goals.

If a female coworker feels envious or competitive with us,
she can make our life miserable at work—even undermine
our career by spreading lies, criticizing our work, or stealing
our ideas. In fact, a great deal of our success or failure at work
can be attributed to whether we are accepted and respected
by our coworkers.

**When your allies are also your enemies, and it feels like
there is no safe place—it may be time to find a safer place
to work.**

Understanding Yourself—
The Key to Change

ᏜᎧ

ONLY BY DISCOVERING the original causes of your behavior can you make permanent changes. Nothing else—not your willpower, not the advice of others, and certainly not self-criticism—will help you until you understand yourself. The encouragements in this section focus on helping you to understand why you are attracted to emotionally abusive people and why you have had a tendency to stay in abusive relationships.

Why Am I Attracted
to Emotional Abusers?

⚭

*What's wrong with me? I can't believe I've done it again.
I thought that this time I had gotten involved with a good
guy, someone who really loved me. But he's just like all the
rest of the jerks I've known. Why do I keep doing this to
myself? When am I ever going to learn? I fall in love
and have high hopes that this person will be the one,
but he never is. I always find out that he's just using me,
like all the rest.*

from *The Emotionally Abused Woman*

This kind of verbal self-flagellation is common among emotionally abused women. We can't understand why we keep getting into emotionally abusive relationships that leave us feeling hurt, angry, ashamed, fearful, confused, and—most of all—stupid.

Instead of mentally beating yourself up for making yet another mistake in your choices of people, it will be far more productive for you to begin looking at *why* you choose abusive people in the first place. The chances are high that you were emotionally, physically, and/or sexually abused as a child, and so you have been programmed to seek out abusive people. In essence, your past has set you up for further abuse.

It is far more beneficial to look for the reasons for your behavior than to constantly criticize yourself for it.

What You Deserve

Gentle and giving—all the rest is treason.

KENNETH PATCHEN

Even if you recognize the fact that you are indeed being emotionally abused, you may still believe that you deserve to be treated in an abusive manner. Many women feel they do not deserve to be treated well. Instead of rejecting those who treat them poorly, they accept the behavior without question. They may be so filled with shame and self-loathing that they believe they don't deserve any better treatment.

Begin to recognize such thinking as a symptom of low self-esteem and of the emotional or other kinds of abuse you suffered as a child. You have been accustomed to being treated with indifference, disrespect, or cruelty, and you may even have come to believe that such treatment is natural.

Women who have been raised in healthy families, on the other hand, expect to be treated with consideration, respect, and kindness, and they reject people who treat them otherwise.

Start to become your own healthy family by treating yourself with kindness, consideration, and respect, and expect others to treat you the same.

Self-Hatred

∞

Sometimes I just hate myself. I don't know why,
but I let everybody walk all over me, my boss, my husband,
my kids, even my friends. I agree to do things I don't want
to do, I go places I don't want to go, and all the while
I resent it. I just can't bring myself to say no to people,
no matter how hard I try.

from *The Emotionally Abused Woman*

This is a typical statement from someone who is being emotionally abused. In addition to all the other damage that emotional abuse inflicts, it causes us to hate ourselves for putting up with it. Time after time we agree to do something and then resent doing it because we realize how unappreciated we are. Time after time we allow someone to take advantage of us, belittle us, or reject us and instead of getting angry with the abuser we get angry with ourselves. We know, deep down inside, that we shouldn't stand for this kind of treatment for one more minute and yet we stand for it for weeks, months, even years.

We must turn self-hatred into self-forgiveness. By learning about the reasons for our behavior, we can begin to understand why we put up with abuse. By understanding that we are just doing what we have been trained to do, we will begin to have empathy for ourselves, to forgive ourselves, and to take steps toward changing ourselves.

Begin to turn your self-hatred into self-forgiveness.

Shame

Debilitating shame is an isolating experience that makes
us think we are completely alone and unique in our
unloveability. It is a feeling that we are intensely and
profoundly unloveable. Debilitating shame is a state of
self-hate and self-devaluation that is comparable to little
else. It makes us feel that life is happening to us and that
we are helpless in the wake of that happening.

JANE MIDDELTON-MOZ
Shame and Guilt

Shame can be a devastating emotion. With each incident of
shaming we feel more unloveable, less significant, more iso-
lated, and more dependent. Emotional abuse can be one of
the most shaming experiences a child can have, whether it is
being told she is unwanted, being humiliated in public,
being disapproved of, being treated as if she is flawed, or
having her boundaries violated.

**I am loveable and important and becoming more and more
independent every day.**

How Do I Change?

The way out is through the door you came in.

R.D. LAING

We must go back to the beginning—to our childhood, to our parents, to those first experiences of deprivation, rejection, and abuse—to find out why we are attracted to abusive people and why we let people abuse us.

Going back into the past can be painful, but it is well worth the journey. No one permits abuse as an adult unless she was abused as a child. It is that simple and that complex. Open your mind to the possibility that the abuse you have recently been through or are suffering today is something you have experienced before. Open your mind to the answers that lie in your childhood history.

Turn around and take a look at where you came from. Then you'll know how to get out of where you are.

Rewriting the Past

∞

Thus, whom we love and how we love are revivals—unconscious revivals—of early experiences, even when revival brings us pain. . . . We will act out the same old tragedies unless awareness and insight intervene.

JUDITH VIORST
Necessary Losses

Women who continually get involved with abusive people may be attempting unconsciously, or perhaps even consciously, to rewrite the past. For example, if we couldn't get our parents to love us, we may become involved with people very much like our parents and try to make *them* love us. We develop patterns of relating to people based on our futile attempts to change what has already happened. Freud called this tendency to reenact our past the "repetition compulsion."

Instead of continually rewriting the past, how about starting a brand new chapter?

Your Original Abuser

∞

With him for a sire and her for a dam,
What should I be but just what I am?

EDNA ST. VINCENT MILLAY

Because most emotionally abused women are indeed propelled into abusive relationships because of the repetition compulsion, reenacting past abuse in a futile attempt to change it, it is important to discover who your original abuser is.

Your original abuser is the person who damaged you the most, who most influenced who you are today. More than likely, he or she was a parent or primary caretaker, someone who had a tremendous impact on you.

Most or all of your major relationships have probably involved someone who is very much like your original abuser. By completing your unfinished business with your original abuser (by acknowledging and releasing your anger and pain), you will be able to choose partners based on their good qualities instead of on their resemblance to the abuser.

Freedom of choice for you lies in being able to choose partners and friends because of their good qualities, not because they remind you of someone else.

Completing
Unfinished Business

∽

THE NEED TO REPEAT THE PAST is a compelling and unconscious drive. Unless you complete your unfinished business, you are destined to continue your pattern of becoming involved time after time with the same kind of abusive person and situation.

The following encouragments will help you in your process of dealing with those repressed emotions, conflicts, and issues that cause you to repeat negative patterns in relationships.

Unfinished Business

∞

Look Back in Anger
JOHN OSBORNE

By allowing emotional abuse to continue you are deepening the wounds from your childhood and avoiding your real work—that of completing your unfinished business. Unfinished business can include any or all of the following: feelings you haven't expressed, things you have left unsaid, false hopes you are still holding onto, and conflicts left unresolved.

While the emotional abuse you suffered as a child will never be washed away completely, by releasing your pain and anger from the past, confronting directly or indirectly those who hurt you, and becoming your own good parent, you will be giving yourself the gift of a life in which you can freely choose who you want to be and who you want in your life.

Nothing is more worthwhile than working to set yourself free of the past.

Repeating the Past

∽

*So we beat on, boats against the current, borne back
ceaselessly into the past.*

F. SCOTT FITZGERALD
The Great Gatsby

Unless we complete our unfinished business from the past
we are destined to repeat it—making the same mistakes,
choosing the same kind of people, experiencing the same
pain over and over.

Repeating the past is like falling down on the same sore
knee over and over. Each time it is injured, the knee gets
weaker and weaker, and with each fresh injury it takes longer
to heal. Similarly, each time we enter into a new relationship that ends up being abusive, we not only experience a
new wound to our self-esteem but the old wounds flare up,
too. Consequently, our self-esteem becomes lower with each
new encounter and it takes longer to recuperate from each
new assault.

We must begin to treat ourselves like the injured people
we really are. Because our self-esteem is weakened, we need
to give it time to heal before exposing it to possible new
injury.

**Don't keep falling down on the same injury. Let the
wounds you have heal, and learn how to play the game
better so you don't have to fall down so often.**

Patterns

*All (life) is pattern . . . but we can't always see
the pattern when we're part of it.*

BELVA PLAIN

We all have developed patterns of behavior that we blindly
repeat time after time, often to our dismay. As mysterious as
these patterns may seem to be—continually getting involved
with abusive lovers, or choosing abusive friends, or always
ending up with an abusive boss—it is important to remember that they really aren't mysterious at all. These patterns
are merely evidence that we have unfinished business from
the past to deal with. The more these patterns are set, the
more unfinished business we need to complete.

**It's time to break your old patterns and start new ones—
patterns based on healthy choices.**

Family

Family faces are magic mirrors. Looking at people who belong to us, we see the past, present, and future.

GAIL LUMET BUCKLEY

Unfortunately, no matter how hard we try not to, we often behave like our parents and make the same mistakes they made. Their influence on us was so great, we almost can't help but repeat their patterns. But in spite of the similarities, we are also uniquely ourselves, and as such we have the chance to make some significant changes in our lives—to break the cyle of abuse once and for all. Just because your mother may have put up with abusive behavior from your father doesn't mean you have to endure abuse in your relationships. When you look in the mirror and see the similarities to your parents, make sure you also see the differences.

You are not your parents, no matter how much of them you see when you look in the mirror.

Childhood

The events of childhood do not pass,
but repeat themselves like seasons of the year.

ELEANOR PARJEON

Childhood is never really over. Because it is by far the most significant time in our life in terms of learning, growth, and the establishment of patterns, it will always remain with us in the form of powerful memories. But our childhood can be over in the sense that we do not have to continually repeat negative patterns from the past.

Part of growing up is letting go of your childhood—not the memories but the behaviors.

Rewards of Truth

I tore myself away from the safe comfort of certainties
through my love for truth; and truth rewarded me.

SIMONE DE BEAUVOIR

Your love of the truth will most certainly take you down a different path than the one the average person follows. And you may end up alone on your path for a while. It will be painful to face the truth about the abuse you suffered as a child, and to acknowledge that because of this abuse you have a tendency to get involved with abusive people as an adult. If you decide to confront your parents about their abusiveness, they may alienate you from the rest of the family. If you confront the abuser about his or her behavior, you may meet with rejection.

But the perpetual lies and deceptions have kept you confused, distorting your reality and causing you to blame and doubt yourself. One of the many rewards of facing the truth is that it will enable you to regain your power and help you to place the blame where it belongs.

While the truth may hurt, it cannot harm me.

Unlearning

∞

The first problem for all of us, men and women,
is not to learn, but to unlearn.

GLORIA STEINEM

Unlearning is like taking out the hem of a dress. You can't remove the stitches too fast or you will tear the material. You have to do it patiently, a stitch at a time. Then, you have to contend with the crease that remains—the memory of the old hem. Painstakingly you must iron out the crease so that the material doesn't curl up where the old hem used to be. If you're not careful and diligent, the material will go back to the familiar crease. It will take a while for the material to adjust to the new hem, but eventually it does.

Anything that is learned can be unlearned.

Relearning

It is best to learn as we go, not go as we have learned.

LESLIE JEANNE SAHLER

How do we unlearn years of negative conditioning and relearn more positive messages? How do we unlearn the role of passive female who allows others to abuse her, and relearn how to be an assertive woman who stands up for herself? We unlearn by refusing to believe all the old negative messages we have received, the criticism and insults we have been bombarded with all our life. We relearn by reminding ourselves daily that we deserve to be treated with respect and consideration and that we never deserve abusive treatment from anyone.

Relearning is harder than learning, but it can be done.

Allowing Yourself
to Express Your Feelings

ↄ◦

Why grieve, when nothing helps?
We cry because nothing helps.

SHELDON KOPP
What Took You So Long?

Victims of childhood abuse typically have a difficult time expressing feelings. This is partly because we are simply not used to doing so. We are accustomed to repressing our emotions, ignoring or minimizing our pain, and hiding how we really feel from ourselves and from others.

But a large part of our identity lies in whatever emotions we are feeling at any given time. Denying our feelings is thus denying a part of our very self, pushing it down and smothering it. Allowing ourselves to express our feelings—whether it be anger, pain, or fear—is an assertion of our right to feel and to be ourselves, an assertion of our true self.

We all have the tendency to want to run away from our feelings. One of the best ways to avoid our emotions is to make sure we are never alone long enough for our feelings to emerge. Once we spend some time alone, we find that our repressed feelings will bubble up and cry out for expression. This experience often frightens us and drives us back out into the world where our feelings get drowned out by the noises around us.

Allowing myself to express my feelings is one of the most important things I can do for my recovery.

Permission to Feel

∽

You were probably taught at an early age that you should suppress and deny your emotions. One or both of your parents may have been cut off from their feelings and were thus unexpressive and unaffectionate. As a child, you may have been told that you were "too sensitive" or "felt too strongly about things." You were probably told that you overreacted to situations. Ironically, you were reacting normally, but your parents felt threatened by your emotional expressions because they tended to avoid their own feelings.

Since you didn't get permission from your family to express your feelings—and probably never will—you need to give that permission to yourself. It will be difficult at first to counter the negative messages you have received from family and society in general, but in time it will become second nature to give yourself permission to feel.

Give yourself permission to feel. Don't wait for someone else to give it to you; you could wait forever.

Fear of Your Emotions

I was afraid that once I started allowing my feelings to surface I wouldn't have any control. I had held them in for so long, I was sure they would just burst out and I'd be like a crazy person! But you know what? I just started letting them out a little at a time, and I was okay!

from *The Emotionally Abused Woman*

We often become frightened when we feel anything intensely, whether it be anger, fear, pain, or even love and joy. We are afraid that our feelings will overpower us or we will go crazy from them. We imagine our emotions spilling out all over the place, creating havoc in our lives.

In reality, it is what we *don't* express that can get us into trouble. The more we repress our feelings, the more likely it is that they will burst out when we least expect it. You will not go crazy if you allow yourself to feel and express your strong emotions. If you consistently allow yourself to express your feelings when they occur instead of holding them in, you will find that you will actually feel more in control of your emotions, not less.

There is far more reason to fear the feelings you hold in than the ones you express.

Reclaiming Lost Emotions

You may be in a state of emotional bankruptcy,
"sleepwalking" through life and depriving yourself
(and others) of any emotionality.

from *The Emotionally Abused Woman*

A great part of the damage caused by any kind of childhood abuse is that it leads us to disown our emotions, to push them down until we are no longer aware of them. You may have learned to disconnect from your emotions as a method of survival during times of chaos or abuse. The emotional and/or physical trauma that you suffered as a child may have been so severe that your body had to shut down in order to protect you from a deluge of pain.

Now it is time to reclaim those disowned emotions, to open yourself up gradually and allow your feelings to peek out. Test the waters gently if you must, choose safe people to expose your tender feelings to, but vow to wake up from your emotional slumber and to join the living.

Sleepwalking can be dangerous. Open your eyes and your heart and begin to feel.

Body Memories

*What you know in your head will not sustain you
in moments of crisis... confidence comes from body
awareness, knowing what you feel in the moment.*

MARION WOODMAN

The most effective way to reclaim all of your emotions—pain, anger, fear, guilt, shame, joy, and love—is to begin to pay attention to your body. Even when you unconsciously repress your feelings, your body remembers them. These memories are called *body memories*. Your body remembers what it felt like when you were neglected, criticized, and rejected as a child. For each emotion, your body experiences a different set of physical sensations. It remembers the pain and anger you felt then with stiffness, constrictions, and tension.

Your body hurts, bleeds, tingles, or tightens for a reason. It is trying to tell you something. It is reminding you of the kinds of childhood trauma you experienced. Listen to your body. Heed its messages.

Now is the time to reconnect with your body, to let it express and release all the pain of childhood.

Uncovering Your Anger

⌒

Now I hope to break through into the rough rocky depths,
to the matrix itself. There is violence there and
anger never resolved.

MAY SARTON
Journal of a Solitude

Uncovering your anger is like digging for gold. It will take a lot of sweat, a lot of struggle, and a great deal of commitment because often you will have to dig very deep with few results at first. But your repressed anger, once found, can be a treasure that provides you with an avenue of healing.

Your anger can provide you with the strength, motivation, and resolve to complete the recovery process and to start your life anew.

Keep digging for your anger. No matter how deep you have to go, it is worth the struggle.

Anger As a Positive Emotion

I tell you there is such a thing as creative hate!

WILLA CATHER
The Song of the Lark

Anger itself is not a negative emotion. It is what we do with our anger that determines whether it is negative or positive. If we go about spewing out our anger on innocent people, our anger becomes negative. If we hold anger in and turn it against ourselves, it becomes negative. But if we find constructive ways of releasing it and safe places to let our anger out, it becomes a positive force in our lives, creating energy, motivation, assertiveness, empowerment, and creativity.

Begin to see the positive aspects of anger.

Fear of Your Anger

∽

I believe that anyone can conquer fear by doing the things
he fears to do, provided he keeps doing them until he gets a
record of successful experiences behind him.

ELEANOR ROOSEVELT

Anger can be the most threatening and frightening of all our emotions. For this reason, victims of abuse have a difficult time accepting and expressing their anger. Your fear of anger has kept you imprisoned in the past, afraid to stand up to those who have hurt you and afraid to go forward. If you can conquer your fear of your anger, you can rise above the status of victim to that of survivor.

Anger is energy, a motivating force that can empower you to feel less helpless. By releasing it you will find that you rid yourself of the physical and emotional tension that has sapped you of energy that you could otherwise use to motivate yourself to change your situation. The more you express your anger, the less afraid of it you will be.

Anger is your way out—take it.

Anger Versus Blame

Anger as soon is fed is dead
'Tis starving makes it fat.

EMILY DICKINSON

While anger is a natural, healthy emotion when ventilated properly, blame is a wasted and negative experience. The difference between anger and blame is that blaming keeps us caught up in the problem, while releasing our anger constructively allows us to work through the problem.

Continually blaming others for what they have done to us keeps us stuck in the past, and we remain emotional children. But when we release our anger in healthful ways (such as writing "anger letters") toward those who abused and damaged us, we are able to step out of blame and let go of the past.

By letting go of blame you are letting go of the past.

The Pain Under the Anger

I imagine one of the reasons people cling to their hatred so stubbornly is because they sense, once hate is gone, they will be forced to deal with pain.

JAMES BALDWIN

As important as it is to recognize and then release our anger, it is equally important to remember that beneath our anger is pain. It is often pain that causes us to become angry in the first place; unless someone hurts us we usually do not become angry with him.

Sometimes we hang onto our anger to avoid facing the underlying pain. If you find that your anger seems to linger on too long, take a peek underneath it to see if pain is hiding there that you have been avoiding. Unless we expose our pain it will never have a chance to heal but will fester and grow more painful every day.

Release your anger and you will expose the pain hiding underneath.

Pain

Pain—has an Element of Blank—
It cannot recollect
When it begun—or if there were
A time when it was not—

EMILY DICKINSON

Pain is a part of life. You can no more expect to get through life without it than you can expect to get through life without breathing. Some of us breathe so shallowly that we scarcely breathe at all, and consequently scarcely live at all. Others take huge, deep breaths, sucking up the air as if it were their last chance, living life to the fullest. Every experience we have, each physical feeling, whether it be pain, or fear, or anger, or love, or joy, is proof that we are alive.

Let yourself feel your pain. Don't be afraid of it. Embrace it. Revel in it. It is proof that you are alive.

Fear

It is not that you must be free from fear. The moment you try to free yourself from fear, you create a resistance against fear. Resistance, in any form, does not end fear. What is needed, rather than running away or controlling or suppressing or any other resistance, is understanding fear; that means, watch it, learn about it, come directly into contact with it. We are to learn about fear, not how to escape from it, not how to resist it through courage and so on.

J. KRISHNAMURTI

The only way to deal with fear is to admit we are feeling it and then allow ourselves to experience it. Instead of trying to talk ourselves out of our fear, we need only face it. Hidden or ignored, fear tends to grow to gigantic proportions, becoming a huge monster in our imaginations. But faced head on, fear tends to diminish and eventually slink away with its tail between its legs.

Face your fear. It usually isn't as frightening as it appears.

False Hope

For we cannot climb into a time machine,
become the long-gone child and get what we want
when we oh so desperately wanted it.
The days for that getting are over, finished, done.

JUDITH VIORST
Necessary Losses

A major part of completing your unfinished business with your original abuser(s) consists of letting go of any false hope that you will ever get from him what you didn't get as a child, or that you can undo what has already been done.

You also need to acknowledge that no one else is going to come along and bestow on you what you so longed to get from your parents. You must mourn the loss of your childhood, the loss of your "fantasy" parents, and the loss of any false hope of getting now what you didn't get then.

Let go of your false hope so you can make room for real hope.

Confronting Your Original Abusers

◯◯

Daddy, daddy, you bastard, I'm through.

SYLVIA PLATH
"Daddy"

Confrontation is different from releasing your anger.
Although part of your confrontation will undoubtedly
include releasing your anger, your primary purpose is to stand
up to those who have hurt you, to tell them how they hurt
you and how you feel about them. Confrontation is a way of
resolving or bringing closure to the relationships that plague
you most: those with your parents and other childhood
abusers. Once you have expressed these feelings, you are
bound to feel better about yourself; you may even feel better
about the relationship.

Confrontation provides you an opportunity to set the
record straight, to communicate what you need from these
people now. Confronting those who have hurt you gives you
a chance to resolve the most important relationships you
will probably ever have.

**Confront your original abusers and you will begin to put
the past behind you once and for all.**

Forgiveness

Children begin by loving their parents. After a time they
judge them. Rarely, if ever, do they forgive them.

OSCAR WILDE

Forgiving doesn't mean that you forget or ignore the past but
that you recognize it is possible for a person to change and
begin again. If you are able to forgive the people who damaged you in your childhood, you'll feel a sense of relief and a
new freedom within yourself.

On the other hand, you may discover that your original
abuser is not open to looking at what he did to damage you;
he may even continue to abuse you in much the same ways
he always did. In that case, forgiveness is not always possible.

I will forgive them if I can and forgive myself if I can't.

Becoming Your Own Good Parent

*We have needs we can meet in different ways, in better
ways, in ways that create new experiences.*

JUDITH VIORST
Necessary Losses

Although you cannot expect anyone else to give you what
you were deprived of as a child, you can begin to provide
these things for yourself. Becoming your own good parent,
giving yourself the nurturing and caring that you are still so
much in need of, is an important part of completing your
unfinished business. Once you begin to be your own good
parent, by nurturing yourself, encouraging yourself, and giving yourself positive self-talk, you will be less resentful of
those in your childhood who deprived and neglected you.

**In order to truly let go of the past and stop the yearning,
you must become your own good parent.**

Should You Stay
or Should You Leave?

BEING IN LIMBO—wanting to leave an abusive situation but being afraid to; knowing you should leave an abusive person but desiring to be with him; knowing you need to make a decision but fearing it will be the wrong one—is a horrible predicament. The following encouragements are aimed at helping you get out of your unhealthy state of limbo and make the right decision for yourself.

The Importance of Making a Decision

Action is the antidote to despair.

JOAN BAEZ

At some point, you will need to decide whether you are going to focus your energy on saving the relationship or on preparing yourself for leaving and perhaps ending the relationship completely.

Remaining in a state of limbo can be dangerous to both your physical and emotional health. If you stand with one foot on one side of a huge precipice and one foot on the other, sooner or later you're bound to fall unless you take that step in one direction or the other.

It is very difficult to make a decision you know will affect the rest of your life. But not facing the decision to stay or leave is a decision in itself. It is a decision to let someone else decide for you, to allow life to happen to you instead of you happening to life.

Don't stay in a state of limbo. Take that step. Make life happen.

Choices

*Full maturity . . . is achieved by realizing that you have
choices to make.*

ANGELA BARRON McBRIDE

As trapped, confused, and afraid as you are, it is important to
remember that you do have choices. Often we feel as if we
don't have choices when what we want in the moment is not
possible. But don't confuse having no choices with being disappointed because things didn't turn out the way you wanted.
As soon as you can let go of the need to have things the way
you want them, you will open yourself up for a lot of other
possibilities. Then you will see that your choices are many.

For example, while your relationship may not be a
healthy one, you could choose to enter marriage counseling
to see if the unhealthy aspects of the relationship can be
changed. Or, you could choose to separate temporarily from
your lover or spouse and test the waters to see how you feel
without him. Once you get over the initial shock of separa-
tion, you might be surprised how good it feels to be away
from the continual abuse.

**There is no limit to your choices once you open yourself
up to the possibilities.**

How Do You Decide?

*Does this path have a heart? If it does, the path is good;
if it doesn't, it is of no use.*

CARLOS CASTAÑEDA
The Teachings of Don Juan

We all know deep in our heart when something is right. When a decision is correct we sense the rightness in our heart as a feeling of warmth, swelling, or solidity. When a decision is a good one for us we sense a silent YES! in our heart and feel a surge of power deep inside.

Listen to your heart when you ask the questions. It will tell you what you need to know.

Trusting Yourself

Let me listen to me and not to them.

GERTRUDE STEIN

If you are not willing to trust yourself, other people and events will determine the direction of your life. Begin to listen to your own heart. Follow your passion and trust your inner wisdom, even if it means giving up what is secure and familiar.

Be true to yourself, even if it means losing the approval of others and risking rejection. Be willing to give up what you think you should feel, do, or think in exchange for being who you really are.

Begin to trust that you will do the right thing for yourself and that even if you make a mistake, you'll be okay.

Trusting Hunches

Trust your hunches. They're usually based on facts filed away just below the conscious level.

DR. JOYCE BROTHERS

Often our first feeling or hunch about a situation tells us more than anything else. We need to trust our intuition instead of analyzing or trying to figure out the situation intellectually. Our effort to *understand* someone or something often keeps us trapped in the situation because it keeps our mind spinning and keeps us disconnected from our true feelings.

No one else knows you better than you know yourself; therefore, no one is better equipped to make your decisions. Trust your intuition, your instincts, your hunches, and your body. They will not steer you wrong.

The more you trust yourself, the more your inner wisdom will blossom.

Your Health

Your health is bound to be affected if, day after day, you
say the opposite of what you feel, if you grovel before what
you dislike and rejoice at what brings you nothing but
misfortune. Our nervous system isn't just a fiction; it's a
part of our physical body, and our soul exists in space, and
is inside us, like the teeth in our mouth. It can't be forever
violated with impunity.

BORIS PASTERNAK

Your health is an important consideration when you are
making your decision whether to leave or stay. Emotional
abuse damages both your physical and emotional health.
Emotional abuse cuts to your very core, forming scars that
may be far deeper and more lasting than physical ones. Like
Chinese water torture, each insult, each criticism, each
rejection wears on you until you are bound to crack eventually. You may begin to suffer from physical ailments such as
high blood pressure, ulcers, colitis, headaches, arthritis, asth-
ma, or other stress-related illnesses, or from emotional
disturbances such as depression, panic disorders, suicidal
thoughts, eating disorders, or sleep disorders.

You may already have begun to suffer from some or many
of these symptoms. If so, I have one question for you: Is it
worth it?

**Warning: Allowing yourself to be emotionally abused is
dangerous to your health.**

Limits

∽

*You never know what is enough unless you know
what is more than enough.*

WILLIAM BLAKE

We all have our limits. Others may have criticized you because you have stayed in a destructive relationship so long, and you certainly have been critical of yourself. But just because your limits are not the same as those of others around you doesn't mean you don't have any limits. You know when enough is enough for you. The important thing is that you not go past your own limits, not that you abide by the limits of others.

I will honor my own limits and learn when enough is enough.

Risking

And the trouble is,
if you don't risk anything,
you risk even more.

ERICA JONG

Risking can be a frightening thing, yet at the same time it can be exciting. It's all in the way you look at it. There are basically two kinds of risks: gambling risks and calculated risks. If you think of risking as a game—sometimes you lose and sometimes you win—it takes some of the fear out of the process. But if you perceive it as putting your life on the line, you will be terribly frightened and will probably not take risks at all. Few risks are actually life-threatening, however.

Calculated risks on the other hand are really not risks at all but more like plans of action based on careful consideration. Deciding to leave a destructive relationship is a calculated risk. You don't have much to lose and everything to gain.

If you don't take the risk of standing up to an abuser or leaving an abusive situation, you risk even more—more abuse, more damage to your self-esteem.

True Love or False?

In real love you want the other person's good.
In romantic love you want the other person.

MARGARET ANDERSON

We often confuse romantic love with real love. Romantic love is when we feel we absolutely *must* have someone or we will die. It is when we need the other person so much that life seems absolutely empty without him.

Real love, on the other hand, is expansive, open, and trusting, not restrictive, withholding, and possessive. It is not based on need but on a desire to give the person we love the space and encouragement to be the best he can be; in the process we become the best we can be. When we genuinely love someone and feel loved, we become the best version of ourselves that is possible, and so does our partner.

True love brings out the best in us. Romantic, needy love brings out the worst.

Obscssive Love

*Looking back, I realize that my loves were, in actuality,
obsessions. They caused me more pain than pleasure.
Sometimes, I can't distinguish between pain and ecstasy.*

HENRY MILLER

Obsessive love does indeed cause us more pain than pleasure. Real love is easy, gentle, kind, and giving. Obsessive
love is difficult, rough, cruel, and taking. When we love
obsessively we are not loving a real person at all but a fantasy, an illusion, or a projection. We want to possess this
illusion because we know how fleeting it is.

No one can hold onto a fantasy.

What Is Love?

∞

Using another as a means of satisfaction and security is not love. Love is never security; love is a state in which there is no desire to be secure; it is a state of vulnerability.

J. KRISHNAMURTI

It's sometimes difficult to distinguish love from need. We may think that because we feel as if we can't live without someone, we must love him very much. But this is more a sign of need than love. If our sense of security is based on another person, if our happiness seems to depend on whether that person is available to us, the chances are that our feelings stem from neediness rather than true love.

When we are already whole, secure people, finding someone to love is like the icing on the cake. We don't need him in order to have a happy life, but our love sure makes life a lot better. Unfortunately, most people look to love to make them whole, to fill up some empty space inside themselves.

Love is like the icing on the cake. Unfortunately, most people think of love as the bread and butter that they can't live without.

Sharing Laughter

We cannot really love anybody with whom we never laugh.

AGNES REPPLIER

Many abusive people have no sense of humor, particularly about themselves. They take themselves far too seriously to ever laugh at their own mistakes or inadequacies. Instead, they laugh at us, taking obvious pleasure in our mistakes and shortcomings.

How wonderful it is to be able to laugh together with someone, to share the pleasure and healing power of laughter, to almost fall down from laughing so hard, to cry tears of laughter together.

I deserve to surround myself with people who can laugh at themselves and laugh with me instead of *at* me.

Taking a Stance

⁢○◯⁢

Standing in the middle of the road is very dangerous; you get knocked down by traffic from both sides.

MARGARET THATCHER

There are only two circumstances that will stop an abuser from continuing his abusive behavior. The first, and most significant, is when an abuser recognizes that he is abusive and needs to change. Unfortunately, most emotional abusers are unwilling to examine themselves honestly; they have an investment in making their victims feel responsible for any problems in the relationship.

The second circumstance is when the victim refuses to put up with any more abusive behavior. Taking this stance will require you to make a commitment to yourself that you are no longer willing to tolerate abuse and that you will let your abuser know this.

Standing up to the abuser is frightening, but it's your only chance for a healthier relationship.

The Six Months Test

∽

If you had only six months to live, what would you do,
and if you're not doing that now, why not?

STEPHEN THOMAS

One way to decide whether you should leave is to ask yourself, "What if I had only six months to live? Would I stay or leave?" Your answer could provide some interesting insights.

If you had only six months to live would you want to spend it with the abuser? If your answer is yes, how would you like to spend the time? Would you want to spend it fighting, crying, being angry, feeling guilty, or feeling rejected, or would you want to spend it peacefully, happily, in playful enjoyment? Is that really possible with the abuser?

If you wouldn't want to spend the last six months of your life with the abuser, you shouldn't be with him now.

Telling Yourself the Truth

∽

We know the truth, not only by the reason,
but by the heart.

BLAISE PASCAL

If you are really honest with yourself, you will realize that
you already know the truth about your situation. You know
what is best for you—you know whether you should continue the abusive relationship or not. When you hide the truth
from yourself, you choose to deliberately withhold something from yourself that will provide you with a tremendous
amount of good in the end. Lying to yourself or trying to fool
yourself is an act of self-betrayal.

Don't betray yourself. Let your heart tell you the truth.

Being Angry with the Truth

The truth will set you free. But before it does,
it will make you angry.

JERRY JOINER

Nothing makes us more angry than to discover the truth about something and realize that it changes everything. The reason we tend to be so good at fooling ourselves, minimizing the abuse and making excuses for the abuser's behavior, is that deep down we know that once we admit we are indeed being emotionally abused and we recognize how damaging it is to us, we will be forced to change the situation.

Like the woman who suspects her husband of cheating but doesn't really want to know because the knowledge will force her to act, we may not really want to know we are being abused. Denial often lulls us into a false security, while the hard truth is like a cold shower or a slap in the face.

As much as you may hate the truth, it is a wake-up call.

What Price Are You Paying to Stay?

∞

No partner in a love relationship… should feel that he has to give up an essential part of himself to make it viable.

MAY SARTON

No matter how afraid you are of being on your own, no matter how insecure you are about anyone else ever loving you, you must begin to ask yourself, "What price am I paying to stay in this relationship?" If the price you are paying for a little bit of security is your self-esteem, it isn't worth it. If the price is your very self, in the sense that you can't be yourself for fear of being ridiculed, insulted, or rejected, then the price is way too high.

Nothing—I repeat, nothing—is worth the loss of your self or your self-esteem, because without these things you are nothing.

Compromise

Don't compromise yourself. You are all you've got.

JANIS JOPLIN

To compromise means to adjust or settle by mutual conces-
sion or a blending of two different things. This means that
sometimes one party gets his way and sometimes the other
does, and sometimes they find a solution that pleases them
both. To emotionally abused women, however, compromise
tends to mean that they always give in to what the other
person wants. Seldom do they ask for or expect others to
give in to their needs. They fool themselves into thinking
that they don't need much, and they don't believe anyone
would want to give to them even if they did ask.

**Stop sacrificing your own needs for those of others. Your
needs are just as important.**

Pretending

When one is pretending the entire body revolts.

ANAÏS NIN

What a price we pay for pretending to be someone we aren't—for pretending that we are happy when we aren't, that we want to do something when we don't, that we are interested in something when we aren't, that we appreciate advice when we don't. We are seldom ourselves, because we assume others wouldn't like us if we were.

We often pretend so much that we lose track of our real selves. We pretend to feel things, to the point that we don't know how we really feel. We pretend to care about others so much that we forget who we really care about. We pretend to be someone else so much that we forget who we really are.

Stop pretending and you may discover who you really are.

Accepting Second Best

∽

If you lower your standards you deserve everything you get.

THOMAS MELOHN

Many women have such low self-esteem that they feel they have to settle for what they can get. They believe they are so unattractive, so stupid, so incompetent, or so helpless that they can't get anyone better than the abuser.

This, of course, is exactly what the abuser wants you to believe and probably what he tells you daily. "You're lucky to have me because no one else would put up with you." "You're so stupid (fat, ugly, sexless, etc.) that no other man would want you." These are the kinds of insults emotional abusers use to keep you insecure and keep you under control.

As difficult as it is to believe right now, you are not as ugly, stupid, incompetent, or helpless as the abuser would have you believe. As soon as you are able to leave the abusive situation, you will begin to see things more clearly and recognize yourself for who you really are.

Don't settle for second best, especially if it means putting up with abusive behavior.

Fear of Change

I have accepted fear as a part of life—specifically the fear of change. . . . I have gone ahead despite the pounding in the heart that says: turn back.

ERICA JONG

We are all afraid of change. Change evokes the fear of loss and abandonment, a sense of insecurity and chaos. We fear we will regret our decision to change and long for the way our life used to be. But a funny thing happens as we change: the things we cherished so much before are often overshadowed by our new life; our losses are soon forgotten as we gain new insights and new ways of living and as we let new people into our life. Instead of looking back on our old life longingly, we usually end up appreciating the positive differences the change has made.

Since you can't see ahead to envision all the positive changes your decision to leave will make in your life, you will need to rely on a certain amount of faith.

I have faith that the changes I am making will lead to good things in my life.

Metamorphosis

It seems necessary to completely shed the old skin before the
new, brighter, stronger, more beautiful one can emerge....
I never thought I'd be getting a life lesson from a snake!

JULIE RIDGE

We certainly can learn a lesson from the snake. The snake,
like us, goes through a tremendous change, but unlike us, he
doesn't do it struggling and screaming. Quietly and peacefully he lets nature take its course.

As painful as shedding our old skin is, it is necessary. We
cannot start a new life without letting go of the old one, otherwise we'd be carrying around too much baggage. Let your
old life slide off you and let yourself become who you were
meant to be.

**Be like the snake and let your metamorphosis occur quiet-
ly and peacefully, the way nature intended it to.**

If You Decide to Stay

IF YOU DECIDE TO STAY IN YOUR RELATIONSHIP or situation, you will need to begin doing a number of things in order to make the relationship healthier. The following section will encourage you to communicate your needs better, to stand up to the abuser and let him know you are not going to allow his abusiveness any longer. They will also help you to stop rescuing others and to establish better boundaries.

Working to Change the Situation

∽

Nobody can make you feel inferior without your consent.

ELEANOR ROOSEVELT

Choosing to stay in an abusive situation does not mean you have to continue being abused. No matter what your reason for staying, you will need to continually work on yourself to avoid this.

If you decide to stay you must begin to change the situation by speaking up for yourself, by letting the abusive person know that you will no longer tolerate mistreatment. Otherwise you are setting yourself up for more abuse, more pain, and most important, more damage to your self-esteem.

You can't afford any more emotional damage. The more abuse you allow, the worse you feel about yourself.

Assertiveness

If I'm too strong for some people, that's their problem.

GLENDA JACKSON

Being assertive does not mean being aggressive, pushy, or selfish. It means being able to state your views and desires directly, honestly, and spontaneously, to act without indecision, and to be true to yourself. Being assertive means simply being able to state clearly and calmly how you feel and what your needs are.

I can assert myself and still respect the feelings and rights of other people.

Standing Up for Yourself

The longer you allow the abuser to get away with mistreating you, the more he will continue to do so. While I am not inferring that you are in any way responsible for the abuser's behavior, it has been found that abusers lose more and more respect (if they ever had any) for the women who allow the abuse to continue. A typical abuser will take your silence and compliance as permission to continue to abuse you or even to escalate the abuse, because he knows you will not stop him.

If you don't stand up for yourself, no one else will.

Speaking Up

I am the woman who holds up the sky.
The rainbow runs through my eyes.
The sun makes a path to my womb.
My thoughts are in the shape of clouds.
But my words are yet to come.

POEM OF THE UTE INDIANS

Many people get confused about the purpose of speaking up. They feel that unless the other person accepts their point of view, their effort was wasted. However, the purpose of speaking up is not to change the other person's point of view, but merely to assert yours. In some sense, it doesn't matter whether the other person even hears you, much less whether you persuade him. What matters is that you are able to speak your mind, that you do not squelch your ideas and feelings. Once you begin to assert yourself without any expectations, you will gain more self-esteem and the courage to continue speaking up.

It doesn't matter whether anyone but me hears my words. I will begin to speak up because my words are important.

The Courage to Be Angry

*Courage is resistance to fear, mastery of fear—
not absence of fear.*

MARK TWAIN

It takes courage to admit that you are angry rather than to hide anger. It takes courage to face the person you are angry with directly and risk the consequence of rejection or retaliation rather than to get back at him indirectly, vengefully, or manipulatively. It takes no courage to push the anger down and pretend you don't care. That is the safe but unhealthy way out.

Ironically, the more you take the risk of being angry, the braver you will become. Your anger will give you the courage and strength you need to continue standing up for yourself.

Be brave enough to be angry and your anger will empower you and make you even braver.

Expressing Your Anger

∽

I was angry with my friend;
I told my wrath, my wrath did end.
I was angry with my foe;
I told it not, my wrath did grow.

WILLIAM BLAKE

Since you have decided to stay, you need to get rid of your anger so that you can begin the relationship anew with no old resentments and grudges. If this relationship is going to have a chance to work, you must express the anger that you have felt for so long toward the abuser. Repressed anger can become a tremendous burden, causing you to withdraw from your partner and making you unable to be truly open. Unless you release it once and for all, your pent-up anger will keep seeping out and contaminating the relationship.

If you're going to start over, start fresh with no old resentments and anger poisoning the relationship. Get them out in the open.

True Strength

∽

True strength is delicate.

LOUISE NEVELSON

Most people think that strength is hard, tough, and inflexi-
ble. But true strength is soft, vulnerable, and pliable. The
strongest tree is the delicate willow that bends with the wind
so as not to break.

You don't have to resist and scream and puff yourself up
to be strong. True strength comes from the inside out, starting with a belief in yourself, your own sense of what is right,
and a personal commitment to yourself to honor your own
feelings.

**Be like the willow in the storm, bending but refusing to
break.**

Differentiating the Past
from the Present

∞

You can never plan the future by the past.
EDMUND BURKE

Your current abuser may be constantly pushing your buttons and reminding you of the past and of your original abuser. It will help you to feel less intimidated by him if you don't mix him up with your original abuser.

As much as your current abuser may be like your original abuser, he is not him. Work on making that distinction and you will find that your relationship will be a lot smoother.

You cannot hold your current abuser responsible for what your original abuser did.

Learning to Communicate

∽

Trouble is a part of your life, and if you don't share it,
you don't give the person who loves you
enough chance to love you enough.

DINAH SHORE

In order to have a good relationship, both people must learn how to communicate openly and honestly about their troubles, feelings, needs, likes and dislikes, and hopes and dreams. Each person needs to be a partner to the other by being willing to listen and able to give honest feedback, being able to comfort without smothering, and being encouraging without controlling. If you decide to stay in the relationship, you and your partner will need to learn how to communicate in ways that insure that each of you is heard by the other.

I will take the risk of communicating with my partner about my troubles, feelings, my likes and dislikes, and my dreams.

Learning to Take Care of Yourself

∽

I have another duty equally sacred . . . My duty to myself.

HENRIK IBSEN
A Doll's House

Because of all your prior conditioning, you may believe that taking care of yourself is a selfish act. But your highest responsibility is to yourself. When you take care of your own needs first, you will be able to be a genuinely caring, giving person, not a martyr thinking everyone owes her something or a victim begrudging all that she gives. Although it will be uncomfortable at first, and you may be afraid that others won't like you unless you cater to their needs first, keep trying. Eventually, you will find that nothing bad happens to you just because you think of yourself first or because you do what *you* want to do.

I have an obligation to myself and to others to take care of my own needs first.

Healthy Boundaries

∽

There's something magical about reaching that point of being ready to set a limit. We know we mean what we say; others take us seriously too. Things change, not because we're controlling others, but because we've changed.

MELODY BEATTIE
The Language of Letting Go

Most of us start a relationship thinking we have certain limits in terms of what we will or won't tolerate from the other person. But as the relationship progresses, we tend to move our boundaries back, giving in more and more until we end up tolerating things we had meant to reject and doing things we were determined not to do.

The people around you need to know you have boundaries. Begin to set limits on what you will allow others to do to you and what you will allow yourself to do for other people.

Stick to your boundaries and enforce them. Mean what you say and say what you mean.

Stop Giving Yourself Away

I believe that what woman resents is not so much giving
herself in pieces as giving herself purposelessly.

ANNE MORROW LINDBERGH

As women we are raised to be care-givers instead of care-receivers as men are. From an early age most of us learn to derive a great deal of our sense of self and our self-esteem from giving to others. We tend to give pieces of ourselves away until we have little or nothing left. We need to start saving some of ourselves for ourselves, giving to ourselves in the same way we so generously give to others. Begin listening to yourself, comforting yourself, and providing for yourself instead of giving it all away to others.

In order to share myself, I have to have a self to share.

Stop Rescuing

We are the rescuers, the enablers. We are the great
godmothers to the entire world. We not only meet people's
needs, we anticipate them. We fix, nurture, and fuss over
others. We make better, solve, and attend to. And we do it
all so well. "Your wish is my command," is our theme.
"Your problem is my problem," is our motto.
We are the caretakers.

MELODY BEATTIE
Codependent No More

Rescuing or enabling is not an act of love. We don't rescue
because we love; we rescue because we want to gain a false
sense of control over someone else. We rescue because we
are repeating a pattern from childhood as a way of avoiding
our feelings of helplessness. We rescue because we assume
the other person can't handle the responsibility of his own
feelings, because we can't tell the truth, because we can't say
no, or because we are afraid the other person will get angry
with us. And, most important, we rescue because we don't
feel good about ourselves.

The best thing you can do for yourself and your partner
or friend is to back off and let him take care of himself.
Leave him alone to face his feelings and suffer the consequences of his actions.

Stop rescuing others and start rescuing yourself.

Patience

∞

"I think patience is what love is," he said, "because how could you love somebody without it?"

JANE HOWARD

Patience and love go hand in hand. When we love someone we are patient with him. We don't constantly criticize him because he isn't perfect; we know he is trying as hard as he can.

However, we need to learn the difference between patience and tolerating too much. Generally, we put up with too much in relationships, letting people walk all over us. Being patient with someone we love means that we don't expect more than the other person is capable of and that we give the other person plenty of time to grow and change and to learn from his mistakes. Tolerating too much means that we hang in there even when the other person has shown us time and time again that he has no intention of growing or changing.

The person I need to be most patient with is myself.

If You Decide to Leave

Even though leaving an abusive relationship or situation may be one of the best things you've ever done for yourself, it will nevertheless be painful. The following encouragements will help you to survive the pain, gain strength from it, and go on with your life in spite of it.

Leaving

∽

I used to believe that anything was better than nothing.
Now I know that sometimes nothing is better.

GLENDA JACKSON

Leaving is always difficult. You may be saying goodbye to someone you love, or a job you enjoy, or a friend you care about, but you are also saying hello to a healthier way of living and a brighter future. We often have to make a space in our lives in order for the good things to find a resting place. Otherwise, we find that when the good things come along we are so busy with the negative in our lives that we don't have room for the positive.

Nothing can be better than something, especially when that something is negative.

The Strength to Leave

All serious daring starts from within.

EUDORA WELTY

It takes strength to leave an abusive relationship. Walking away from abuse not only takes strength but gives strength. The abuser has been sapping your energy day in and day out, week after week. Getting out from under the tyranny, criticism, and rejection, you will feel a tremendous burden lifted. You'll be surprised how much strength you'll feel when you're not weighed down by abuse.

Strength comes from doing what is best for yourself, from taking care of your own needs instead of expecting others to, from loving yourself even when you think no one else does.

I have the strength I need to leave and stay away from the abuser.

Saying Goodbye

∽

You must do the thing you think you cannot do.

ELEANOR ROOSEVELT

Our lives are full of doing things we think we cannot do. When you were a child, you thought you'd never master riding a two-wheeler—but you did it. Later on, when you were learning to drive a car, you thought you'd never be able to make a left-hand turn in a busy intersection—but you did it. Now, we are talking about doing something far more difficult: leaving your abusive lover, friend, or situation. Just as you were able to do all the other things in your life that at first you thought you couldn't do, you will surprise yourself by doing this one, too.

Do the thing that is painful now and you will save yourself much pain in the future.

Mourning the Loss

Between grief and nothing I will take grief.

WILLIAM FAULKNER
The Wild Palms

Someone recently told me she felt bad because she was robbed of the gift of mourning. I had never heard mourning described that way, and for a moment it caught me off-guard. But within minutes I knew exactly what she meant. Having recently lost my mother, I knew both the joy and pain of the grieving experience. To think of missing that experience feels like a greater loss than the loss of my mother.

Grief is one of the range of emotions that make us human. It is good to feel, no matter what the emotion, for it connects us to our humanity.

Don't deny yourself the gift of grief.

Tears

There is a palace that opens only to tears.

ZOHAR

Even though it may feel as if the pain will never end, it eventually will—not all at once but gradually, a teardrop at a time. So let the tears come, let the healing begin. Allow yourself to feel the pain of your loss, to cry all the tears you need to cry, to feel the pain of your broken heart, for only by doing so can your heart mend.

Nothing, not even pain, lasts forever.

Sorrow

I saw sorrow turning into clarity.

YOKO ONO

Through sorrow comes wisdom and vision, insight and strength. Sorrow is like a heavy cloud that descends suddenly and hovers over us for a long time. But as surely as sorrow befalls us, a wind will eventually come and blow the cloud away, providing us with a clearer view of our life.

Let your sorrow be like the wind, clearing the air and providing you a much better view.

Getting Past the Pain

The cure for anything is salt water—
sweat, tears, or the sea.

ISAK DINESEN

While this quote may seem overly simplistic, I don't think it is. Think about it. We have known for years about the physical and even the emotional benefits of exercise and physical labor. Exercise helps ease depression, tension, and anxiety, so why not the emotional pain of loss? And because tears have been found to have healing qualities beneficial to both the body and the soul, crying has long been thought to be therapeutic. Last but not least, let's not forget about the healing qualities of the ocean—the powerful yet calming sea.

So cry, go for a walk, work in your garden, clean house. When all else fails, go to the ocean and let the waves wash away your pain.

Bathe yourself in your sweat, your tears, and the ocean. Take the "cure."

Emptiness

∽

When the mind soars in pursuit of the things conceived in space, it pursues emptiness. But when the man dives deep within himself, he experiences the fullness of existence.

MEHER BABA

Because of your low self-esteem, you, like many other emotionally abused women, have been searching for something outside yourself to give you a sense of completion and a sense of being worthwhile. Like many women in our culture, you have probably looked to romantic love as the solution for your feelings of incompleteness and inadequacy. But no one can complete you, fill up your emptiness, or give you a sense of meaning but yourself.

If you give yourself the time and space to get to know yourself and your feelings, you'll find that you can fill up the emptiness a layer at a time. Each time you allow yourself to feel a feeling, each time you allow yourself to express an emotion, you are filling up another empty space inside.

Fill up your emptiness with yourself—with your emotions, your desires, your beliefs, and your dreams.

Asking for Help

The healthy and strong individual is the one who asks for
help when he needs it. Whether he's got an abscess
on his knee or in his soul.

RONA BARRETT

There is no disgrace in asking for help, only in needing help
but refusing to reach out for it. We all need help now and
then. Anyone who tells you he never needs help probably
needs help more than you do. So reach out for help if you
feel confused, depressed, or overwhelmed. Reach out for
help and you'll be surprised how much help there is.

**Asking for help is not an admission of weakness but of
humanness.**

Growth Through Pain

You will not grow if you sit in a beautiful flower garden,
but you will grow if you are sick, if you are in pain, if you
experience losses, and if you do not put your head
in the sand, but take the pain and learn to accept it,
not as a curse or punishment but as a gift to you with
a very, very specific purpose.

ELISABETH KÜBLER-ROSS

There is always a gift of wisdom that comes with pain. We may not understand the gift until long after the pain has subsided, but we have received it nevertheless.

Instead of envying the happiness of others, instead of looking longingly at couples who seem to be happy, realize that you have something to learn from your situation. You have an opportunity to grow from it and become a far better person. Don't waste it envying the contented ones in the flower garden.

Appreciate pain as the gift it is—an opportunity for growth.

Lessons from Pain

∞

*We tend to think of the rational as a higher order, but it is
the emotional that marks our lives. One often learns more
from ten days of agony than from ten years of contentment.*

MERLE SHAIN

When we are content we tend to grow sluggish and lazy. But
when we are in pain we become alive, aware, and alert. Each
moment becomes poignant, each breath important. We suddenly see things we have been ignoring, we suddenly hear
things we have deadened our ears to. Our pain becomes so
intense that life itself becomes intense. In these times of
poignancy and intensity, we learn. We learn the lessons that
we have been avoiding or have been too stubborn or too lazy
to learn. We learn that all the wisdom of the ancients is
indeed true, and we learn it firsthand.

**Savor the poignancy of your pain and learn its lessons.
They are the most important ones you'll ever learn.**

Overcoming Your Pain

∞

Although the world is full of suffering,
it is also full of the overcoming of it.

Many, many people before you have suffered, and many have overcome their suffering, including the wonderful woman who said the words above. Helen Keller never gave up and never gave in to her physical handicaps. Think of her example, and the examples of the thousands of others who overcome suffering and hardships every day. Gain strength from their perseverance, gain hope from their victories.

You can and will overcome your pain, but first you have to feel it.

Letting Go

Three words were in the captain's heart. He shaped them
soundlessly with his trembling lips, as he had not breath to
spare for a whisper: "I am lost." And, having given up life,
the captain suddenly began to live.

CARSON McCULLERS
Reflections in a Golden Eye

Letting go hurts. There's just no way around it. It hurts to let
go of old, familiar ways, no matter how unhealthy they are. It
hurts to let go of people in your life who have represented
some form of security, even if they were also abusive. It especially hurts to let go of false beliefs about yourself. But no
matter how painful letting go can be, it can also be incredibly
rewarding and immensely satisfying.

Letting go also means relinquishing the limitations that
have held you down. Letting go of people in your life who
have been abusive opens the door for healthier people to
come in. And letting go of false beliefs about yourself allows
you to truly know your real self. When seen in this light, letting go can be an extremely positive thing.

Only by letting go can you start over.

Alone Again

To be alone is to be different, to be different is to be alone.

SUZANNE GORDON

Many women feel that becoming single again is a fate worse than death. They view it as moving backward or as a sign of failure. For some reason, being alone in our society makes many women feel like rejects, unwanted by anyone. How sad that such a natural state, that of being single, has come to mean such a negative thing. Being single means only that you aren't married—nothing else. It doesn't mean that you are not desirable, or loving, or interesting. There is no shame in being alone. In fact, being alone can be a wonderfully blissful state once you have come to like and respect yourself and learned to enjoy your own company.

I will focus on the positive aspects of being alone instead of the negative ones.

Fear of Aloneness

∽

After 17 years of marriage you're single again,
I don't care how many awards you have and how much
money, it's terrifying.

JANE FONDA

As victims of emotional abuse we have become so convinced that we have nowhere else to go, that no one else could possibly want us, that we stay in abusive situations. Our ultimate fear is that of being alone. The idea of being alone is extremely frightening to those who don't have a good sense of self. For some of us, being alone makes us feel like an abandoned child in a cruel world with no one to turn to—much the way we felt when we were children in an abusive household.

It is important to remember that even though you may feel like a child left alone, you are in fact a woman who, believe it or not, has the strength to face her aloneness and to triumph over it. Remind yourself of this daily and being alone won't be so frightening.

If you can face your aloneness and triumph over it, you will never have to be afraid of being alone again.

Loneliness

Hear that lonesome whippoorwill?
He sounds too blue to fly.
The midnight train is whining low,
I'm so lonesome I could cry.

HANK WILLIAMS

Loneliness can be incredibly painful, an aching in the heart, a mourning of the soul. Missing someone you love is the most painful feeling of all. Nothing can soothe you, nothing can distract you. You want what you have lost and nothing else will do.

But there is a difference between feeling lonely and feeling *empty*. There can be a tremendous poignancy to the feeling of loneliness, an intensity of emotion that is the opposite of the feeling of emptiness. At least when we are feeling lonely we are feeling our *self*—our pain, our aloneness in the world. As long as we are feeling our self and our emotions, we are okay. It's only when we are feeling empty that we are in danger.

Embrace your loneliness and let it remind you that you are alive and feeling.

Freedom From and Freedom to

Freedom breeds freedom. Nothing else does.

ANN ROE

Although you are alone, you are also free. For so long now
your life has been dictated by what someone else wanted you
to do or to be. Now you can begin to do what you want, to
be who you want to be. Now you have the freedom to discover who you really are. Now you have freedom *from* the
oppression, rejection, or abuse you have been living under,
and freedom *to* explore your deepest self, your secret desires,
and your wildest fantasies.

What a wonderful gift!

**Appreciate this freedom for the wonderful gift that it is—
an opportunity to explore your deepest self, your secret
desires, and your wildest fantasies.**

Hope

"Hope" is the thing with feathers—
That perches in the soul—
And sings the tune without the words—
And never stops—at all—

EMILY DICKINSON

No matter how much pain you are in, there is always hope. It may be buried inside you, so deep that you sometimes cannot find it, but it is always there. Sometimes we need to do some excavation before we find hope; it can be covered over with pain, disappointment, and anger. But within us all lies the potential for hope, deep within our soul, singing a quiet tune.

Listen carefully and you will hear the song of hope, no matter how faint.

Taking Time for Yourself

IT IS VERY IMPORTANT THAT YOU DISCOVER who you are, separate from *any* relationship. You've been hiding from yourself by getting lost in one abusive relationship after another, and now you need to take some time to put your life in perspective, to heal from your past relationships, and to do some inner reflection. As scary as the prospect may seem, you need time alone to discover who you really are, to learn to rely on yourself, to learn to like your own company, and to break your tendency to be dependent on others. The following encouragements will help you do all of these things.

Time to Be Alone

*We need time to dream, time to remember,
and time to reach the infinite. Time to be.*

GLADYS TABER

Taking the time to be alone will help you gather the courage
to leave an abusive relationship, to deal with your emotions
after you've left, to avoid abusive relationships in the future,
and to discover what you want and need out of life. From
this position you will be less needy, less desperate to attach
yourself to someone.

This time you take to be alone now may be the only time
you have ever stood alone, not depending on anyone else to
help hold you up. Your fear of being alone has propelled you
into continually seeking relationships and staying in destructive ones. You need to know that you can be alone and be
happy with yourself. That way, you will never stay in any
relationship again out of fear of being alone.

**Giving yourself time alone gives you time to feel, time to
remember, time to just *be*.**

Self-Discovery

*How many cares one loses when one decides
not to be something, but to be someone.*

COCO CHANEL

All of us travel through life with only one constant companion, and that is ourself. How sad if our closest companion is
someone we don't even know.

Spend some time discovering just who you are—what
your likes and dislikes are, what your dreams and aspirations
are, and most important, how you feel.

**At this point in my recovery, there is absolutely nothing as
important as taking this time out for self-discovery.**

Facing Your Aloneness

Millions of persons long for immortality who do not know
what to do with themselves on a rainy afternoon.

SUSAN ERTZ

It is amazing how few people can stand to be truly alone
with themselves. When we are alone we tend to distract ourselves with television, radio, talking on the telephone—
anything rather than confront our own feelings and
thoughts, anything rather than face even for a moment our
aloneness in the world.

Begin by trying to be alone without any kind of distrac-
tion for just five minutes. Notice how difficult it is to silently
listen to your own feelings and thoughts without trying to
run away from them. You'll be amazed at how much can
happen inside you in five minutes. As you discover that the
feelings that emerge do not destroy you, gradually you will be
able to increase the amount of time you are able to be alone
with yourself.

**If you begin to face your aloneness five minutes at a time,
soon you'll know what to do with yourself on a rainy
afternoon.**

Alone with What You Feel

*Anna was saying to herself: why do I always have this
awful need to make other people see things as I do? It's
childish, why should they? What it amounts to is that I'm
scared of being alone in what I feel.*

DORIS LESSING
The Golden Notebook

Just because no one else feels like you do at any given time
doesn't mean your feelings are invalid. Just because someone
doesn't agree with your point of view doesn't mean you are
wrong. Any particular emotion or perception that you have
is valid just because it *is*. No one needs to agree with you
and no one needs to experience a situation the way you do.
Give yourself permission to have unique feelings and perceptions and to value them as much as if hundreds of people
were sharing them. Only by doing this will you free yourself
from the tyranny of being controlled by the opinions and
perceptions of others.

**Begin to value your feelings and perceptions even if no
one agrees with you.**

Finding Your Safe Place

∽

Each person has his own safe place—running, painting,
swimming, fishing, weaving, gardening. The activity itself
is less important than the act of drawing
on your own resources.

BARBARA GORDON

We all need a safe place, a place where we can go to any time
of day or night and know beyond a doubt that we are safe
from harm. For some people this haven is somewhere inside
themselves, a place they go to in their minds. For others, it is
a physical location—a room in their house, their bed, or a
place in nature such as a park or private hideaway.

Find your safe place and go there whenever you feel the
dangers of the world are creeping too close. Go there whenever you become overwhelmed with your emotions, or when
memories come to haunt you.

Whenever things get rough, just think of your safe place
and remind yourself that you will be there soon.

Alone with Nature

Take long walks in stormy weather or through deep snow in the fields and woods, if you would keep your spirits up. Deal with brute nature. Be cold and hungry and weary.

HENRY DAVID THOREAU

Many people find that being alone with nature is the most healing, productive time they can spend. Away from the distractions of their household, away from other people, they are free to connect with themselves and with nature in a profound way. Being alone with nature can help you achieve a different perspective on your problems and come away with a deeper appreciation for the things that are truly important.

Being not only *in* nature but *with* nature is like allowing a cool breeze to wash over your mind, body, and soul, cleansing them and infusing them with new energy.

Give yourself the gift of nature. Bask in it, get lost in it, lavish yourself on it.

The Joys of Being Alone

*What a lovely surprise to discover how un-lonely
being alone can be.*

ELLEN BURSTYN

Very few people have discovered the joys of being alone with
themselves, for few have been willing to go through the pain
to the other side. But once you have discovered that you can
survive the initial feelings of loss and abandonment, overcome the ridiculous stigma of "being alone," make friends
with yourself and become comfortable with your own company, you will discover a joy beyond belief. What a
wonderful feeling to know that you truly do not *need* to be
with someone in order to be happy—that you can be with
yourself and enjoy life to the fullest. What a thrill to realize
that you are enough; that your own reactions, feelings, and
thoughts are interesting, entertaining, and full enough to
satisfy you.

I am enough. Just me.

Solitude

She would not exchange her solitude for anything. Never again to be forced to move to the rhythms of others.

TILLIE OLSEN

Solitude. This word has come to be music to my ears, a word that should be uttered in a beautiful, melodic whisper: s o l i - t u d e. I love the feel of the word as it tiptoes from my mouth.

It hasn't always been this way. Solitude once meant loneliness to me, as it does for so many people. It seemed frightening and desperate, something to be avoided at all costs. But that was before I discovered the true meaning of the word. Solitude is being alone by choice, being alone for the purpose of replenishing the soul, letting the luscious quiet bathe you. It is a time for contemplation, for digging deep into your soul.

Learn to appreciate solitude for what it is—a way of renewing the body, mind, and soul.

Looking Within

∞

What lies behind us and what lies before us are tiny matters compared to what lies within us.

RALPH WALDO EMERSON

No matter what has happened to you in the past and no matter what still lies ahead for you, the most important thing is what lies within you. You can withstand anything, whether in the past, present, or future, as long as you are connected to your *self*—your emotions, what is in your heart, and who you are at your core.

Spend more time looking inside yourself and less time looking into the past or the future.

The Journey Within

∞

I hoped that the trip would be the best of all journeys:
a journey into ourselves.

SHIRLEY MacLAINE

Think of the self-discovery process as an adventure or a long journey. You have everything you need for your trip. Your emotions are your compass, your personal history is your map. And what an experience the journey into yourself can be—full of surprises, new and exciting places, and jam-packed with learning. What better journey could there possibly be?

Allow yourself to explore new paths, new avenues of awareness. There is no end to the things you can discover about yourself—new talents, abilities, and feelings you never knew existed within you.

The journey within is the most important journey you will ever take.

Finding Yourself

∞

One's own self is well hidden from one's own self: of all mines of treasure, one's own is the last to be dug up.

FRIEDRICH NIETZSCHE

Because all your life people have been telling you who you are and what your motivations are for doing the things you do, because you have lost yourself in your attempts to please others, because you've tried to be what you thought others expected you to be, you haven't had a chance to discover who you really are. Now is the time.

Begin to dig up your own treasures instead of envying or emulating those of others. Begin to uncover the layers of self-doubt and fear that have prevented you from discovering your true self.

Finding myself is far more important than finding a new lover.

Journal Keeping

When I don't write, I feel I lose my fire and my color.
It should be a necessity, as the sea needs to heave,
and I call it breathing.

ANAÏS NIN

By keeping a journal in which you record your feelings, innermost thoughts, and dreams, you will likely discover more about yourself than you ever imagined possible. You will discover ideas and feelings long buried, solutions and alternatives to problems, new ways of looking at things, and—most important—new ways of looking at yourself.

Keeping a journal is like taking your pulse and blood pressure—it gives you a good idea of what shape your heart is in.

Fear of the Truth

> ∞

I am never afraid of what I know.

ANNA SEWELL

Why do we fear the truth so much? It is a puzzling question, because we also crave the truth. In reality, we probably fear the unknown more than we fear the truth. In fact, there is a sense of calm that comes over us when we discover the truth, no matter how painful. When the truth is finally revealed we normally feel a tremendous relief, as if we had been holding our breath for a long time and we are finally able to let out a sigh of relief.

Don't fear the unknown, for that is where the truth lies.

Facing the Truth

∞

You never find yourself until you face the truth.

PEARL BAILEY

We tend to hide many things from ourselves—things about our parents and our childhoods, about the people we have become involved with, and, most important, about ourselves. Often these truths hurt us or force us to let go of false hopes and illusions, so it makes sense that we wouldn't want to face them. But as long as we hide the truth from ourselves, we will never truly know ourselves, never discover our purpose in this world. As much as truth hurts, it also liberates and frees.

Being totally honest with yourself is extremely difficult. But without self-honesty there is no self-knowledge.

The pain of the truth will pass, but the pain of ignorance and self-deception continues forever.

Your Relationship with Yourself

∞

*I don't need a man to rectify my existence. The most
profound relationship we'll ever have is
the one with ourselves.*

SHIRLEY MacLAINE

Believe it or not, it is possible to feel complete and whole
without another person. As you continue to develop a self,
you will discover that you no longer need another person to
complete you, to make you feel secure, loved, or validated.
You will be able to enjoy your own company more and more
and be less often in need of others to ward off fear of aloneness or to make you feel less empty. You will begin to provide
for yourself an inner sense of security and validation instead
of looking for it outside yourself. And you will begin to love
yourself so much that you will not depend on others to make
you feel loveable.

**I do not need another person to complete me. I am a
whole and loveable person in my own right.**

Taking Back Yourself

*How hard it is to escape from places! However carefully
one goes, they hold you—you leave little bits of
yourself fluttering on the fences, little rags and
shreds of your very life.*

KATHERINE MANSFIELD

The price we pay for flitting about from relationship to relationship, frantically looking for someone to take responsibility for us, is that parts of us get scattered all over the place and we lose ourselves. That is why you must stop giving yourself away so easily and so quickly, and why you must now spend some time alone gathering up the rags and shreds of your life—gathering up your self.

Don't keep giving yourself away. You're all you've got.

Assessing the Damage

*I came to see the damage that was done
and the treasures that prevail.*

ADRIENNE RICH
Diving into the Wreck

Just as the captain of a ship assesses the damage after a storm, now is the time for you to take a long, hard look at what this last abusive relationship has done to you. Making an honest assessment of the damage can help remind you not to allow anyone else to emotionally abuse you again. It will also help you to know which areas of recovery to focus on.

Along with assessing the damage, make sure that you acknowledge the parts of yourself that are still intact, the assets you retain. The abuser did indeed take a lot from you, but he didn't take everything. You still have your integrity. You still have your emotions (no matter how buried). And you still have yourself.

No matter how much the damage, there are still treasures buried deep inside.

Self-Knowledge

You can live a lifetime and, at the end of it, know more about other people than you know about yourself.

BERYL MARKHAM

How true this statement is and how ironic. The one person we should know the best is, of course, ourself. And yet we tend to spend more time and energy trying to understand others. It would seem that one of our major goals in life should be to know ourself as much as possible by the end of our life.

If we spent half as much time paying attention to what makes us tick as we do to what motivates other people, we'd not only have a much better self-understanding, but we'd also have a lot more time for further self-exploration.

The self-knowledge you gain by opening inward can be profoundly gratifying. Get in touch with your own inner guidance and begin to listen to and heed the messages of your heart and body.

It is far more important to know yourself than to know anyone else in the world.

Getting to Know Yourself
Through Your Feelings

∞

Cruelty has a human heart,
And Jealousy a human face;
Terror, the human form divine,
And Secrecy, the human dress.

WILLIAM BLAKE

One of the best ways to discover who you are is to focus on what you feel. Only by knowing yourself through your emotions can you grow to trust yourself, your perceptions, and your thoughts. Give yourself permission to feel and to express to yourself and to others all of your emotions. Each time you deny a feeling, you deny a part of your *self*. Express your fear, hurt, anger, joy. Each time you hide your feelings, you alienate yourself not only from others but from your *self*.

Your emotions are the key that unlocks the door to yourself.

Searching

As long as one keeps searching, the answers come.

JOAN BAEZ

It may seem that you will never understand yourself, and the reasons for your behavior, or discover the answers to many other questions that plague you. Yet if you keep your mind open and if you really want the answers, they will come. They might not take the form you were expecting, and they might not be the answers you wanted, but they will indeed appear.

Your answers may appear in the form of dreams or a sudden insight. They may arise from an inner knowing or from a memory. Just keep your searchlight beaming and focused ahead as you continue your journey. It's bound to illuminate exactly what it should.

Keep your mind open for the answers and they will appear.

Your Inner Self

∞

Let the counsel of thine own heart stand.

ECCLESIASTES 37:13

What a powerful force the inner self is. While we are often not aware of it for long periods of time and while we often suppress it, this force is nevertheless always there inside us, like a tiny voice in the wilderness. When we stop and listen to its guidance, we experience a deep sense of personal fulfillment. When we don't listen, we experience frustration and a sense of emptiness. Open the doorway to your inner world and discover your hidden resources, find answers to questions long unanswered, and receive inspiration and wisdom that will guide you through even the roughest crisis.

Stop and listen to the guidance of your inner voice. It will never steer you wrong.

Going Deep into Yourself

∞

It always comes back to the same necessity: go deep enough and there is a bedrock of truth, however hard.

MAY SARTON

Most of us have several protective layers or facades that serve to conceal our true selves from both ourselves and others. In order to truly know ourselves we must strip away these facades and go deep within.

This process can be likened to an actor's role in a play. At the end of a play we must remove our costume, wig, and stage make-up. But even when we are free of all the physical trappings of the role, we must still work mentally to step out of the character we were playing and come back to our true self.

Dig past your facades and protective barriers and uncover your true self.

Finding Your Bliss

I feel that if one follows what I call one's bliss—the thing that really gets you deep in the gut and that you feel is your life—doors will open up. They do!

JOSEPH CAMPBELL

The phrase "follow your bliss" speaks to many people even if they are not really sure what it means. We *intuitively* know what it means; we *feel* the meaning deep inside. We connect with our bliss when we are totally immersed in our work or in a favorite creative or recreational activity. We experience our bliss when we have followed a hunch about something and find that we were correct—when we honor a gut feeling and later find out that our intuition was telling us something important. In fact, our most successful choices in life come not from following the pull of other people, events, or other outside forces, but from heeding certain promptings from deep within.

As you learn to follow your heart and trust your inner voice more often, as you begin to allow yourself to explore who you are and what pleases you, you will find that you will experience your bliss more and more often.

If you are looking for direction, look no further. Follow your bliss. Follow your heart.

Being Yourself

*Something we were withholding made us weak
Until we found it was ourselves.*

ROBERT FROST

It would seem that "being oneself" would come naturally and easily. After all, who else are we going to be? But ironically, being oneself can be one of the most difficult things a person can do. From the time we were small children, most emotionally abused women have been discouraged from being ourselves and instead encouraged to be what others expected us to be.

Now is the time to begin to be exactly who you are instead of who you think you should be. It's a big risk, of course, because from time to time others will be disappointed in you if you don't meet their expectations. But the rewards are far greater than the risks.

The more you hold your real self down, the harder it is to be yourself. Trying to be what others expect you to be depletes your energy, while being yourself energizes you. You are not weighed down by the extra burden of pretense and facade.

Trying to be someone else or trying to be what someone else wants you to be drains you of your energy. Being yourself gives you strength.

Explaining Yourself

∽

"I can't explain myself, I'm afraid, Sir," said Alice,
"because I'm not myself, you see."
"I don't see," said the Caterpillar.

LEWIS CARROLL
Alice's Adventures in Wonderland

What an incredible statement Alice was making. So often
we attempt to explain our behavior to others when we don't
really understand it ourselves. Conversely, if we are truly
being ourselves we find that not only is it easier to explain
ourselves to others, but we feel less need to do so. When we
are being authentic—meaning that we are being true to our
basic nature—we are far more capable both of communicating with others and of realizing we don't need to justify
ourselves to anyone.

Be yourself and you won't have to explain yourself.

Remaining Yourself

∞

You were once wild here. Don't let them tame you!

ISADORA DUNCAN

Once we discover our true self, and find our bliss, the next challenge is to *continue* being ourselves. Like a wild animal that has been captured and tamed and then set free, in the same way for us it is difficult to recapture our basic nature and then remain true to it. At every turn people will try to persuade us to be someone else—to meet others' expectations and needs, to be more like them, to conform to the roles society expects of us.

It will take a great deal of determination and courage on your part to remain steadfast to yourself—to your goals, your beliefs, and your basic nature. But after working so hard to find yourself, you won't be so quick to give yourself away or to lose yourself again.

Stay true to your nature, even if it means you stay a little wild!

Self-Forgiveness

∽

If you haven't forgiven yourself something,
how can you forgive others?

DOLORES HUERTA

Self-forgiveness can be the most difficult form of forgiveness to achieve, but it is one that we must strive for at all costs. If we don't forgive ourselves for our real or imagined transgressions, we will continue to bring people into our life who will punish us. We need to forgive ourselves for being attracted to emotional abusers, for allowing emotional abusers to damage us, for staying in abusive situations even when we knew we should get out, for blaming ourselves for the abuser's behavior, and, most important, for not taking care of our own needs.

You may never be able to forgive the abuser or your family for victimizing you, nor are you required to do so in order to recover. But recovery does depend on you forgiving *yourself*.

Self-forgiveness is not optional, it is essential. It is an act of humanity, self-care, and self-love.

Making Peace with Yourself

∞

Until you make peace with who you are, you'll never be content with what you have.

DORIS MORTMAN

At some point in life we need to accept ourselves the way we are. Sure, we want to become the best we can be, but we do not achieve this by constant self-criticism. One of the best ways of meeting our potential is through self-acceptance, which in turn builds self-esteem. By becoming content with who we are and with what we have, we are freed from empty, endless striving. By achieving a certain level of self-acceptance we can make peace with ourselves. Paradoxically, this inner peace will in turn motivate us to continue striving to be the best we can be.

By making peace with yourself, you'll find you are far more motivated to keep striving to make yourself the best you can be.

A New Start

∽

*I decided to start anew—to strip away what I had been
taught, to accept as true my own thinking. This was one of
the best times of my life. There was no one around to look
at what I was doing, no one interested, no one to say anything about it one way or another. I was alone and
singularly free, working into my own, unknown—no one
to satisfy but myself. I began with charcoal and paper and
decided not to use any color until it was impossible to do
what I wanted to do in black and white. I believe it was
June before I needed blue.*

GEORGIA O'KEEFE

You, like Georgia, may have never known a time when
someone wasn't scrutinizing you, casting a critical eye to
make sure you weren't doing something wrong. At first it
can feel unnatural and strange to realize that there is no one
to answer to but yourself. But believe me, soon it will feel
incredibly good. Once you really "get it" that you are
absolutely free to do anything you want without having
someone's critical eyes glaring at you, once you savor the
freedom of being totally on your own, you will feel as if you
can soar like a bird.

**Throw out all your colors and start anew. That way you'll
find out what colors you really like.**

Differentness

I didn't belong as a kid, and that always bothered me. If only I'd known that one day my differences would be an asset, then my early life would have been much easier.

BETTE MIDLER

The world is as fascinating as it is because it is made up of so many different kinds of people. How boring life would be if we were all the same! How terribly sad if we all acted the same, looked the same, felt the same, and believed the same things. It is our differences that provide the world with its charm, its color and vibrancy, its complexity, its beauty. Learn to appreciate your differentness—the things that make you interesting, that make you uniquely you. Don't be afraid to be different, to stand out in the crowd. You'll miss an awful lot of applause if you continue trying to be like everyone else.

I am a unique person and my differentness is what makes me interesting and exciting.

Learning to Rely on Yourself

Just remember, we're all in this alone.

LILY TOMLIN

As hard as it is to fully acknowledge the fact, we all come into the world alone, die alone, and essentially live all the days in between alone. That doesn't mean we cannot share some meaningful, fulfilling, and intimate times with those we love along the way, but it does mean that we are the only constant, the only person we can rely on to be there no matter what.

Unfortunately, all too often we let ourselves down by not taking care of ourselves, by ignoring our true wishes and desires, and by subjugating our needs to those of others. We must begin to meet our own needs, understanding once and for all that no one else is going to take responsibility for us. As unbearable as the task may seem, we must learn to take care of ourselves.

The price we pay for not shouldering our own burdens is that we eventually lose the strength to hold ourselves up.

Treating Yourself Well

CO

Treat yourself at least as well as you treat other people.

THEODORE RUBIN

Part of the emotional abuse you are suffering from is the neglect you have subjected yourself to. Emotionally abused women tend to focus too much of their attention on the needs of others. Much of the time that we should devote to caring for our own needs and nurturing ourselves, we spend instead taking care of others. We often do this in an attempt to force others to take care of us. It is like we are making an unspoken bargain: "I'll take care of you so that you will take care of me."

Learning to take care of yourself will not be easy, but you can do it. As a child you were probably not taught to take care of yourself, nor were you encouraged when you did so. Because of your prior conditioning, you may think that taking care of yourself is a selfish act. But self-care does not mean you stop caring about others; it just means you *start caring more about you*.

Now is the time to acknowledge how important your needs are and how important *you* are.

Raising Your Self-Esteem

THE ENCOURAGEMENTS in the following section are aimed at helping you raise your self-esteem. You will be encouraged to stop being self-critical, to give yourself more praise, to work on self-acceptance, to stop letting others define you, and to begin nurturing yourself.

Your Level of Self-Esteem

∽

We drive through life with our brakes on, and one of those brakes is low self-esteem.

JAMES NEWMAN,
LOS ANGELES COUNTY SELF-ESTEEM
TASK FORCE CHAIRMAN

Nothing is as important to our psychological well-being as our self-esteem. Our level of self-esteem affects virtually every aspect of our lives. It affects how we perceive ourselves and others, and how others perceive us. It affects all our choices in life, from what career we pursue to whom we get involved with. It affects our ability to both give and receive love and our ability to take action when things need to be changed. It affects our ability to be creative. It affects our stability. It affects whether we are followers or leaders. It certainly affects whether we allow someone to abuse us or not.

Self-esteem is how a person feels about herself; it is her overall judgment of herself. If we have high self-esteem, we have an appreciation of the full extent of our personality. This means that we accept ourselves for who we are, with both our good qualities and so-called bad ones.

Raising your self-esteem means learning to accept who you are rather than trying to change or trying to create a whole new you.

Change

∞

*Many people seem to feel that change in one's self-concept
can come about smoothly. This is not true in any
person. . . . When we learn something significant about
ourselves and act on that new learning, that starts a wave
of consequences we can never fully anticipate.*

CARL ROGERS

Changing one's ideas about oneself is extremely difficult. We
tend to hold onto ideas about ourselves, even negative ones,
because it is so frightening to begin to see ourselves differently. Once we change our ideas about ourselves, once we
see ourselves in a different light, nothing else about our lives
remains the same.

Why is this the case? As we view ourselves differently,
other people will begin to see us in a different way and then
treat us accordingly. Some people will feel threatened by our
changes, but most will begin to treat us in more respectful,
appreciative ways. We'll also find that we cannot go back to
the way we were before, even though we may long to do so
at times when we feel insecure.

**When you begin to change your ideas about yourself, be
prepared for the earth to move.**

Self-Criticism

It is hard to fight an enemy who has outposts in your head.

SALLY KEMPTON

Beyond a doubt, the most important thing you can do to raise your self-esteem is to stop being so critical of yourself. Your low opinion of yourself was caused to a great extent by others having been critical of you in the first place. Your self-esteem has been chipped away by parents, siblings, schoolmates, friends, lovers, and bosses. Criticism from others has developed into a lifelong pattern of being self-critical, which has constantly reinforced your low self-esteem.

When you are being self-critical, you are doing the same thing to yourself that your parents and others have done to you—you are damaging your self-esteem. Don't perpetuate the damage. Build yourself up instead of tearing yourself down. Begin by noticing how many times a day you are self-critical and try to turn those negative messages into positive ones.

Make sure you aren't your own worst enemy. Pay attention to what you tell yourself when no one else is around.

Unconditional Self-Love

❧

The ultimate lesson all of us have to learn is unconditional love, which includes not only others but ourselves as well.

ELISABETH KÜBLER-ROSS

Unconditional love, while probably impossible to fully achieve in this lifetime, is a wonderful ideal to strive toward. The idea is that if we can love someone no matter what he does, if we can love someone freely without placing demands on him, then we experience the bliss of true love.

The same holds true for ourselves. If we can love ourselves just as we are, with no expectations and no demands, we can achieve the heights of self-love and acceptance.

Try loving yourself just as you are, without placing any demands on yourself to be any way except how you are.

Self-Acceptance

*The curious paradox is that when I accept myself
just as I am, then I can change.*

CARL ROGERS

Quite a paradox, isn't it? Yet it is true that the more we accept who we are, with all our shortcomings and faults, the more capable we will be of changing. One of the reasons for this is that the more self-critical we are, the less motivation and confidence we have to change the very things we are critical of.

Instead of judging yourself harshly for your shortcomings, try giving yourself the same benefit of the doubt that you probably give others when they aren't perfect. Try giving yourself half as much understanding as you have given all the abusive people in your life.

If you really want to change, try accepting yourself just as you are. Right now. Today.

Learning from Your Mistakes

There are no mistakes, only lessons.

NEW AGE JOURNAL

It makes a lot more sense to learn from your mistakes than to beat yourself up emotionally because you made them. Those who chastise themselves for their mistakes often feel defeated and have little or no motivation to try again.

On the other hand, those who use their mistakes as lessons find that they are a lot more willing to try again, realizing that they have some valuable experience under their belt this time around.

Learn from your mistakes. Don't let them be an excuse to quit.

Experience

You gain strength, courage and confidence by every experience in which you really stop to look fear in the face.
You are able to say to yourself, "I lived through this horror.
I can take the next thing that comes along."

ELEANOR ROOSEVELT

There is no such thing as *bad* experience or *good* experience. Experience is what makes us who we are. It is what gives us substance, depth, and soul.

Our lives can be compared to the creation of a quilt. In order to make an interesting quilt, we need to gather a wide variety of material and then piece it all together to form an interesting pattern. We don't have to like every single piece of material; it is not the individual pieces that stand out when the quilt is completed, but the entire pattern.

Embrace your experiences, whatever they may be, because they make up the rich tapestry of your life.

Laughing at Yourself

⌒⌒

*When we can begin to take our failures nonseriously,
it means we are ceasing to be afraid of them. It is of
immense importance to learn to laugh at ourselves.*

KATHERINE MANSFIELD

Laughing at ourselves does not mean that we deride and
make fun of ourselves, but that we don't take ourselves so
seriously that we can't see the humor in the fact that we all
make mistakes.

When we get to the place where we can laugh at our
shortcomings and mistakes, we have taken a tremendous
step toward recovery. Being able to laugh at ourselves means
that we are no longer so self-critical, no longer expecting
perfection from ourselves; and we are able to forgive ourselves our mistakes.

**If you can laugh at yourself and not take yourself too seri-
ously, you will find that you aren't quite so afraid of
failure.**

Self-Praise

There be none of Beauty's daughters
With a magic like thee;
And like music on the waters
Is thy sweet voice to me.

LORD BYRON

Not only were you probably overcriticized when you were a child, you were probably also underpraised. Begin now to give yourself the praise you missed as a child. The regular use of self-praise builds self-confidence and validates your real worth. Talk to yourself lovingly, approvingly, reassuringly. Consistently give yourself praise, recognizing the good you have accomplished, just as a nurturing parent would. Support yourself with statements like "Hey, look how well you handled that!" or "I believe in you—I know you can do it."

Begin to give to yourself the praise you have so longed for from others.

Accepting Yourself as You Are

Everything in life that we really accept undergoes a change.
KATHERINE MANSFIELD

Very little of what makes you who you are today was under your control. You had no say as to what genes you would inherit, who your parents were, or how they were going to treat you. Most certainly, the emotional abuse you sustained as a child was not under your control. Your parents emotionally abused you because they had been emotionally abused children themselves or because they had low self-esteem. They were cruel, angry, neglectful, indifferent, and controlling because of their own problems. You did not cause these problems, nor did you cause your parents to be abusive to you by any of your actions.

It is crucial that you recognize that your low self-esteem, your tendency to get involved with abusive people, and all the other symptoms of emotional abuse are not your fault. This is a big step toward learning to accept yourself for who you are today.

Forgive yourself for the things you've had no control over in the past and begin to take responsibility for your choices in the present.

Loving Yourself

Love yourself first and everything else falls into line.
You really have to love yourself to get
anything done in this world.

LUCILLE BALL

Self-love is a healing force for recovery from emotional and physical wounds. The more you love yourself, the more you will be healed from the devastating damage to your mind, soul, and body caused by emotional abuse. Caring for yourself, cherishing yourself, and treating yourself with tenderness—the countless ways in which self-love is expressed—will contribute to your positive feelings about yourself, which in turn will help raise your self-esteem.

Cherish yourself and treat yourself with the kind of tenderness you would show a child.

Taking Care of Your Body

∽

If anything is sacred the human body is sacred.

WALT WHITMAN

Self-nurturing includes taking care of yourself physically. Many women who were emotionally abused are tremendously disrespectful of their body's needs. They tend to load their body with unhealthy food, alcohol, or drugs (including nicotine). They may drive themselves relentlessly, refusing themselves adequate rest and tension-releasing exercise. This is understandable, because many of us were never taught to respect and love our bodies. We probably learned instead to abuse them by watching those around us abusing theirs.

As an adult you may have continued this pattern. In your attempts to repress your uncomfortable emotions, you may have abused your body even further.

Begin to take care of your body by appreciating it for getting you this far—for withstanding all the abuse and neglect it has undergone. Ask yourself why you would want to punish a body that has been so good to you—that carries you through the day, enables you to work, to play, and to experience pleasure. Think instead of repaying your body for its loyalty and strength by rewarding it with healthier food, exercise, and rest.

Taking care of your body is an important step toward loving yourself and toward raising your self-esteem

A Nurturing Environment

*The great law of culture is: Let each become all
that he was created capable of being.*

THOMAS CARLYLE

Valuing yourself includes valuing your time, your energy,
your body, and your worth. You deserve to be treated well by
yourself and by others. Without a healthy image of yourself,
you will not be motivated to practice healthier attitudes and
behaviors. For this reason you need to become your own
nurturing parent, giving yourself the care and support you
missed as a child. Surround yourself with those who are supportive of you, and begin to weed out those who are
unsupportive, unloving, or overly critical. This nurturing
environment will help you to build up a positive image of
yourself and will increase your self-esteem.

**Valuing yourself means creating a nurturing environment
for yourself in which you are treated well by yourself and
by others.**

Joy

Joy seems to me a step beyond happiness—happiness is
a sort of atmosphere you can live in sometimes when
you're lucky. Joy is a light that fills you with hope
and faith and love.

ADELA ROGERS ST. JOHN

Joy is one of the basic emotions, like love, anger, fear, pain,
and guilt. It is as natural and as important as the others, and
yet we probably experience joy less than any other emotion.
The reason for this is that we seldom "find our bliss" or pursue those things that tap into our inner longings and desires.
Thus, we miss out on experiencing this wonderful counter-
part of happiness or contentment.

Now is the time to begin to discover what gives you
joy—what kinds of work, hobbies, activities, and people
make you feel so good that you feel filled with hope, faith,
and love. It *is* possible to have moments of pure joy, intima-
tions of how intensely felt a life can be.

Give yourself the gift of joy.

Changing Your Pattern
and Breaking the Cycle
of Abuse

GAINING INSIGHT INTO YOUR PARTICULAR PATTERN and making the connections between your past and your present have helped you to understand yourself and your motives better. However, because the unconscious drive to repeat the past is so compelling, you cannot expect yourself to change overnight. You need to be vigilant so that you can short-circuit your old patterns as they reappear.

Breaking the cycle of abuse is a lifelong effort, both in terms of your not attracting abusive people into your life and of your not becoming abusive to your children or other people. Don't expect perfection. You will make many mistakes along the way. But if you are truly committed to not being abused and not being abusive, you can be the person who breaks the cycle of abuse in your family. The following encouragements will help you.

Breaking Your Pattern

∞

*Just because everything is different doesn't mean
anything has changed.*

IRENE POTER

It is difficult to begin making healthier choices, whether it
be in the choice of lovers, friends, jobs, or ways of behaving.
It is hard to break habits and start doing things in a different,
healthier way. We tend to be far more comfortable with the
old, familiar—albeit negative—patterns.

It is tempting to continue to wear an old, comfortable
pair of shoes, but we know that eventually we must buy new
ones. As uncomfortable as the new ones may be at first, we
trust that they will eventually become more comfortable the
more we wear them.

In much the same way, in time, your old ways won't feel
so good or so familiar. As you become more and more
healthy and more aware of your negative patterns, the old
ways will begin to feel uncomfortable and unhealthy as new,
healthier habits and behaviors take their place.

**Try on some new ways. They'll be uncomfortable for a
while but soon they'll feel as good as the old ones— maybe
even better.**

The Cycle of Violence

There are people who eat the earth and eat all the people on it like in the Bible with the locusts. And other people who stand around and watch them eat it.

LILLIAN HELLMAN
The Little Foxes

You don't have to stand by and allow abuse to happen—to yourself or to anyone else. That may be what your mother and her mother before her did, but you can break the cycle. You can become the first woman in your family to put an end to emotional and other kinds of abuse, not only by not allowing anyone to emotionally abuse you or your children, but also by making certain that *you* do not emotionally abuse your children—or anyone else, for that matter.

Break the cycle of abuse by not allowing anyone to abuse you and by vowing to never abuse another person.

From Victim to Victor

∞

I am not afraid of storms for I am learning to sail my ship.

LOUISA MAY ALCOTT

Just because you have been a victim in the past doesn't mean you have to continue being one. Begin to stand up for yourself. Speak up for your rights, voice your opinion, ask for what you want, and say what you don't want. Determine that you are not going to be anyone's victim ever again. Begin acting as if you are the assertive, powerful, dynamic person you can eventually become—the powerhouse you have inside you who is just aching to get out!

I am no longer a victim but a survivor, and as such I am courageous, determined, and powerful.

Getting Started

Whatever you can do
Or dream you can,
Begin it.
Boldness has genius
power and magic in it.
Begin it Now.

GOETHE

So often we don't accomplish what we'd like to because we can't get started. Our fear of failure, of not doing something right, or of being laughed at or criticized stops us before we begin. The by-now-familiar culprits are our low self-esteem and lack of a strong sense of self. But somehow we must push past our doubts and fears and begin. It doesn't matter whether we do it the "right" way. It doesn't matter if no one else likes what we've done. What matters is that we have started, and having started we are now on our way.

Don't put off starting for one more day. Begin today.

Adult Choices

*As trapped, confused, and afraid as you are, it is important
to remember that you do indeed have choices.*

THOMAS MELOHN

Victims believe they have no choices. They feel that they
have to go along with others' decisions and desires. When
you were a child, you were a victim of emotional and other
kinds of abuse because you had virtually no control over
your life. You depended on your parents for survival.

As an adult, even when it seems as though you don't
have a choice, you do. For example, you may feel as if you
have no choice but to stay in a job no matter how unhappy
you are, because you need the money. But there may well be
a better job out there if you begin to look. You may need to
go back to school in order to enter a whole new field or to
improve your position.

One thing you have now that you lacked as a child is real
choice. As a child you were bound to your environment. You
could not change your parents, and you could not leave your
parental home. But now, if you do not like what is happening in a particular situation or relationship, you have a
choice—you can leave.

**As a child you did not have a choice; as an adult you do.
Exercise that choice whenever and however you need to.**

Courage

∽

*Courage looks you straight in the eye. She is not impressed
with power trippers, and she knows first aid. Courage is
not afraid to weep, and she is not afraid to pray, even when
she is not sure who she is praying to. When she walks it is
clear she has made the journey from loneliness to solitude.
The people who told me she was stern were not lying:
they just forgot to mention she was kind.*

J. RUTH GENDLER

Courage is indeed kind. It gives us the strength to endure
the most horrendous types of abuse and to triumph over
them. It gives us the will to change those things about ourselves that we once thought unchangeable. It gives us the
power to stand up to those who have been abusive and say
we are not going to take it anymore.

You have shown a tremendous amount of courage in facing the truth about being abused, in looking at the cause of
your attractions to abusive people, and in deciding to do
something about it. It has taken real courage to get this far
in your recovery and to face all the painful truths you have
had to face so far.

**Give yourself credit for being one of those with the
courage to begin the journey and the determination to
stick it out when the pain seems intolerable.**

Freedom

∽

Freedom is what you do with what's been done to you.
JEAN-PAUL SARTRE

As children we didn't have many choices about what was done to us. We were emotionally, physically, or sexually abused by adults who should have cared more for us. We didn't have the freedom to walk away from the abuse, because we were dependent on adults for our very survival. But today we do have freedom—the freedom to walk away from abusive relationships, the freedom to never again enter into another abusive relationship, and, most important, the freedom to heal from both our childhood and adult wounds. Freedom doesn't mean walking away from the past; it means learning from the past and using it as a reminder of where we came from.

Recovery means freedom—freedom to make choices based on what is good for you. It means knowing who you are and what you like. It means once again being able to enjoy your body, your sensations, your relationships, and the feeling of being alive.

Exercise your freedom and determine that you will recover from the abuse you have suffered.

Starting Over

∽

It's never too late—in fiction or in life—to revise.

NANCY THAYER

Starting over—what a wonderful concept. The words sound so encouraging and optimistic. But is it really possible to start over? The answer is yes and no. We can't erase our past and start with a clean slate. But if we think of starting over as beginning a task anew after several false starts, then we certainly can start over.

For example, let's say that you are trying to write a poem. Your first efforts may not please you; you may be unable to say exactly what you intend to say. So, time after time, you pull out a new piece of paper and begin again. After a while you may get frustrated and feel like giving up, but the beautiful thing about it is that there is always another bright white piece of paper available for you to start over with, and each time you try you come closer to writing the poem you want to write.

There's always another chance to revise. Keep trying until you get it right.

Getting Up Once You've Fallen

If you have made mistakes…there is always another chance for you . . . you may have a fresh start any moment you choose, for this thing we call "failure" is not the falling down, but the staying down.

MARY PICKFORD

You are not a failure because your relationship didn't work out or because you once again chose an abusive person to become involved with. You are not a failure because you've had to walk away from an abusive person. The fact that you have had the courage to take an honest look at yourself and your negative patterns, the fact that you have had the courage to start all over again, is evidence of your courageous spirit and your ability to take care of yourself—certainly not qualities of a failure.

Everyone stumbles and falls from time to time. But as long as you get up and brush yourself off and try again, you'll never be a failure.

Happiness

*I don't think that . . . one gets a flash of happiness once,
and never again; it is there within you, and it will
come as certainly as death.*

ISAK DINESEN

Even though it may feel as if you will never experience happiness again, you most certainly will. Happiness is not something that comes from outside but from within. As you continue to grow and change, you will find that happiness will bubble up from within you more and more often, and you will discover that happiness is not limited to romantic relationships.

Happiness may come from experiencing a significant insight about yourself or from a dream that helps you understand something important about your life. Or perhaps it will come in a quiet moment when you realize that you are content to be alone, or in a moment when you feel at one with God or nature. That is what true happiness is—moments of insight, contentment, connectedness. It is when these moments come more and more often that we say we have found happiness.

Happiness will most certainly come again, but it may not come in the forms that you have learned to expect.

A New Life

A woman's life can really be a succession of lives, each revolving around some emotionally compelling situation or challenge, and each marked off by some intense experience.

WALLIS SIMPSON, DUCHESS OF WINDSOR

The idea that women can essentially have several lives within one lifetime has become more and more of a reality. We may experience one life in which we are the helpmate of a husband or mother of our children and another life when that marriage has ended or our children have grown. We can experience one life with one career and another when we choose an entirely different career.

Likewise, we experience one life when we allow ourselves to be emotionally abused, and a remarkably different and better one when we no longer allow such abuse.

This is the beginning of a brand new life—a life free from abusiveness, from rejection and deprivation, a life that is fulfilling and challenging.

New Love

When I was very young I fell deeply in love. . .
and really believed I would never feel that way again. . .
then nine years later. . .I did, and much, much more
strongly and deeply than before.

ISAK DINESEN

Yes, love will come again for you, and this time it can be a
healthier love than you have ever experienced before.
Because you are working on completing your unfinished
business from the past, you will be less attracted to abusive
types. Because you are working to raise your self-esteem and
to take better care of yourself, you will be less likely to stay
in an abusive relationship if you do find yourself in one. And
as you gain more and more of a self, you will be less inclined
to settle for second best in order to avoid being alone.

**Another love will come, and this time you have a real
chance at happiness.**

Spotting Trouble

"Will you walk into my parlor?" said the spider to the fly.

MARY HOWITT
The Spider and the Fly

You probably know the type of abuser you are likely to be attracted to. Be on guard for this kind of person. Even though you know your pattern, you may find yourself drawn to the same abusive type. If you find yourself enormously attracted to someone right away, *beware!* This person is probably the same type of abusive person you have known all your life.

If you feel as though you've known someone for years— you probably have. He is probably a replica of your original abuser(s). Beware.

Taking Time to Get to Know Someone

To fall in love is awfully simple, but to fall out of love is simply awful.

BESS MYERSON

You cannot love someone you do not know. You can be in love with a fantasy or with who you *think* the person is, but you cannot be in love with the real person. Only over time, through observing the person in all kinds of situations and in all kinds of moods, can you truly learn about him.

Too often we get involved with others before we have had a chance to really get to know them. Learn from your past mistakes. Get to know a person slowly, whether it be a new friend or a new lover. You've been through a lot of pain already because you haven't taken your time in becoming involved in relationships. Don't keep inflicting that same pain on yourself over and over.

Don't give your heart away immediately, only to have it broken yet again.

Making Better Choices

A woman has got to love a bad man once or twice in her life, to be thankful for a good one.

MARJORIE KINNAN RAWLINGS

There is certainly something to be said for this philosophy. You may have learned the hard way, but you have indeed learned what it's like to love a bad man. This knowledge can help you pass the next one by and appreciate a good man who will love you for who you are.

In the past, you may have drawn emotional abusers to you like bees to honey. As you let go more and more of your victim mentality, you will not find untrustworthy people so attractive—and, interestingly enough, they will not find you so attractive.

Remember the bad men the next time you want to pass a good one by.

The Urge to Merge

I looked into his face, searching it, trying to find its mystery,
its wonder for me, and I said, almost prayerfully, "If only
I could walk into your eyes and close the lids behind me,
and leave all the world outside."

SHEILAH GRAHAM About F. SCOTT FITZGERALD

We search endlessly for that one true love, that person we
can merge with, the partner who will complete us, that one
special person who will take away our feelings of self-dislike,
desperation, and estrangement. But no two people can
merge, no matter how great the urge to do so, and eventually
we all must face our aloneness. It might as well be now.

**Nothing will give you a sense of completeness but your-
self.**

Individuality

∞

Respect . . . is appreciation of the separateness of the other person, of the ways in which he or she is unique.

ANNIE GOTTLIEB

There is only one you. Out of hundreds of thousands of people, no one thinks exactly as you do; feels exactly as you feel; has the same needs and desires, opinions, goals, preferences, knowledge, or experience as you have. You are uniquely you, an interesting, baffling, complex individual.

Because of this individuality, it is ludicrous to try to merge with another person or to even expect another person to truly understand you or you him. All you can really expect is that you respect each other's differences and appreciate each other's uniqueness.

Respect your own uniqueness and the uniqueness of others.

Real Love

Love from one being to another can only be that two solitudes come nearer, recognize and protect and comfort each other.

HANS SUYIN

This wonderful quote succinctly states what we have been talking about. Real love is not a merging of two souls into one—a coming together—but a coming *nearer*.

Real love is not a smothering love or a possessive love. Real love is loving someone enough that you give each other the gift of trust and space.

You have to be separate enough from someone to really see him.

Intimacy

It all starts with self-reflection. Then you can know and empathize more profoundly with someone else.

SHIRLEY MacLAINE

We cannot be truly intimate with another person until we are able to be intimate with ourselves, and this ability comes from self-knowledge. We must first establish our own identity and know who we are and what we feel, prefer, and want. If we do not know these things about ourselves, we cannot share them with another person. If we are unaware of ourselves, there is no way we can express ourselves to someone else. As we become more and more intimate with ourselves, as we connect with ourselves, we are able to connect in deeper and deeper ways with others.

I choose to be intimate with myself first. Intimacy with others will follow.

Learning to Trust

*When our first connections are unreliable or broken or
impaired, we may transfer that experience and our
responses to that experience onto what we expect from
our children, our friends, our marriage partner,
even our business partner.*

JUDITH VIORST
Necessary Losses

As you continue with your recovery, you will begin to recognize people as their own unique selves instead of as mere shadows from your past. You will be able to really hear what they are saying instead of misinterpreting their words. And you will be able to take in their love instead of pushing it away, negating it, or being suspicious of it.

If you trust others you will occasionally be hurt, disappointed, or betrayed, but if you never trust others you will miss out on experiencing the intensity of intimacy, the tenderness of love.

Trust will come as the shadows from the past subside.

Keeping Your Heart Open

Tears may be dried up, but the heart—never.

MARGUERITE DE VALOIS

You have a heart that is capable of being full of love. But as a child, and later as an adult, your ability to love was corrupted and diminished. Now, as you become healthier, you can reclaim that ability to love and be loved. Now is the time to take down the barriers to your heart. You don't need them anymore.

Until now, you have felt that you needed to close off your heart as a protection against further hurt and betrayal. It is time to start opening up your heart again—opening to love.

Keep your heart open so that the next time love comes your way it will not pass you by.

Getting Used to Healthy Relationships

*I don't know if I'd recognize a healthy relationship if
I saw one. I'm not used to being listened to when I
make a request. I am used to people being defensive when
I have a complaint. And I'm not used to someone actually
changing a behavior so as not to hurt me.*

from *The Emotionally Abused Woman*

It can take a lot of adjusting to get used to healthy relationships. We're so used to chaos and abuse that when a
relationship is going well—when someone treats us with
respect and caring—we sometimes feel like running away, or
running back to those who are familiar, albeit abusive. We
become so afraid that a healthy relationship is "too good to
be true" that we don't give it a chance.

Because of the emotional abuse you have suffered, it is
difficult for you to believe that there are others who can
meet your needs, and that you deserve to have your needs
met. But it *is* possible to have a healthy relationship. If you
give it a chance you'll soon find that the unfamiliar and
frightening will become the norm.

**You won't miss the abuse once you become used to being
treated well.**

Selfhood

∽

*Most lives are a flight from selfhood. Most prefer the truths
of the stable. You stick your head into the stanchions and
munch contentedly until you die. Others use you for their
purposes. Not once do you look outside the stable to lift
your head and be your own creature.*

FRANK HERBERT
Children of Dune

Don't settle for the life of the stable. It may feel safe but it is
too confining. If you stay there you will never discover all
you can be.

Don't allow anyone to fence you in, not even yourself.
Lift your head, stretch your legs, and jump for freedom. Race
through the woods, across the mountains, through the fields.
Feel the wind against your face, feel the strength in your
body. Don't let anyone ever capture you again and try to sad-
dle you. You are a wild thing who needs all of outdoors to
satisfy you.

**You've learned the truths of the stable, now learn the
truths of the open range.**

Continuing to Change

WE DON'T COME TO THE END OF A BOOK or the end
of a time period and decide that we have grown and
changed enough.

Changing and growing will be a lifetime endeavor. If
you take it one day at a time, if you enjoy your experiences along the way and don't focus only on reaching
our destination, you will find that you will come to
enjoy the journey for the journey's sake, growth for
growth's sake.

Continuing to Grow

I think that one's art is a growth inside one. I do not think one can explain growth. It is silent and subtle. One does not keep digging up a plant to see how it grows.

EMILY CARR

The kinds of changes we have been talking about—completing your unfinished business from the past, becoming more assertive, learning to walk away from abusive relationships, discovering yourself, raising your self-esteem, changing your patterns, and breaking the cycle of abuse—all take time, because they all require major changes in your thinking, feeling, and behaving. There is no prescribed amount of time required for each change. Some changes, such as becoming more assertive, may take a relatively short time; others, such as self-discovery, will take a lifetime—but then, you have a lifetime to accomplish them.

Don't keep digging up the plants to see if they are growing. Be patient and trust in the process.

One Day at a Time

*The best thing about the future is that it only comes
one day at a time.*

ABRAHAM LINCOLN

Sometimes we look so far ahead that we don't see the progress we have already made. We attempt to reach such difficult goals that we don't give ourselves credit for all the smaller changes we have made along the way. Recovery results from an accumulation of small transformations rather than one great, sudden change. Small changes can add up to big ones if we acknowledge them and encourage ourselves along the way and if we just take it one day at a time.

The most significant changes occur over time—one day at a time.

Learning

That is what learning is. You suddenly understand something
you've understood all your life, but in a new way.

DORIS LESSING

Learning is a complicated and confusing process at times.
Some things that we should have learned or even things we
have learned to some degree—we have not really learned at
all. Often this happens because we simply are not ready to
learn something. We may need to become stronger before
we can handle the lesson, we may need to be in a safer environment in order to face the truth of the lesson, or we may
simply need more experience before we can learn the lesson
firsthand.

**Lessons are learned when we are ready to learn them, not
before.**

Challenges

∞

Challenges make you discover things about yourself that
you never really knew. They're what make the instrument
stretch—what make you go beyond the norm.

CICELY TYSON

Many people have said that in order to live a full life we must be willing to take risks and make mistakes. But few people talk about how to get to the place where one feels confident enough to take those risks. As emotionally abused women, we understand more than anyone that risks don't come easily when we have low self-esteem and when we have been berated all our life for making mistakes.

We need to start with small risks and gain self-confidence from small victories: being able to live alone, making a new friend, learning to trust our own perceptions. With each small victory we will build up our self-esteem, perhaps enough to try something a little harder later on.

Let others take the big risks. We'll be content with the small, everyday ones—the life-changing ones.

Never Give Up

∞

*When you get into a tight place and everything goes
against you, till it seems as though you could not hang
on a minute longer, never give up then,
for that is just the place and time that the tide will turn.*

HARRIET BEECHER STOWE

How often have you had the experience of feeling as if
you've come to the end of your rope, only to have things
suddenly get better? Whether it's an unexpected check in
the mail, a phone call from a loving, supportive friend offering help, or just waking up in the morning feeling a new
burst of energy or courage, we've all experienced the "tide
turning." So next time you are full of despair, feeling as if
everything is going wrong, remember that things will
inevitably get better soon—they always do.

**Don't give up. The tide will turn if you just hang on a lit-
tle longer. I promise.**

Optimism

No pessimist ever discovered the secrets of the stars,
or sailed to an uncharted land,
or opened a new heaven to the human spirit.

HELEN KELLER

What is optimism? Is it seeing things in an unrealistic, Pollyannaish way? Or is it seeing the glass as half full instead of half empty? I think it is the latter. If the analogy is true that life is a glass that is half full or half empty depending on our perceptions, why not work toward seeing the glass as half full?

There is a difference in the amount of hopefulness we feel when we see the glass as half full, just as there is when we remind ourselves that things truly do get better. If we focus on the negative, we rob ourselves of the hope necessary for change and tend to get caught in a vicious circle of negativity. Focusing on the positive doesn't mean we are unrealistic, it just means we choose to focus our attention on the good things instead of the bad.

If you believe enough and reach high enough, you really can discover the secrets of the stars.

Getting Older

We grow neither better nor worse as we get old,
but more like ourselves.

MAY LAMBERTON BECKER

I've often admired older people who are easily able to stand up for themselves, make their wishes known, and get their needs met with little difficulty. One such person, a woman in her seventies, shared with me what growing older had done for her: "The older I get the freer I get because I just don't worry anymore about what people think of me. It's such a waste of time. At my age I have no time to be coy or diplomatic. People tend to think the old are meek and don't give us the respect we deserve, so I've found that the best way to survive is to just take care of myself and tell people what I want and how I feel and not worry about their reactions."

These are such words of wisdom. I wonder why we have to wait until we are older to begin being more ourselves?

Don't wait until you are old to be yourself. Start today.

It's Never Too Late

∞

It is never too late to be what you might have been.

GEORGE ELIOT

No matter how old you are, it is never too late for you to make your dreams come true or to accomplish the things you have always wanted to achieve. There have been many famous women who didn't start their careers until they were in their forties, fifties, sixties, and even seventies. Think of Grandma Moses and other women who began painting when they were quite elderly. Many women have had second or even third careers, women have had children when they were past their forties, women have fallen in love when they were in their fifties, sixties, seventies, or eighties.

Whatever your dream, don't give up on it because you think you are too old. There is still time to make your dream come true.

There is always time to make dreams come true.

A New Day

∞

Today a new sun rises for me; everything lives, everything is animated, everything seems to speak to me of my passion, everything invites me to cherish it.

ANNE DE LENCLOS

I recently saw a sign outside a church that said, "Even the longest day lasts only twenty-four hours." I stopped and thought for a moment about how true that statement is. Sometimes when we are suffering the time goes so slowly that a moment, an hour, or a day seems endless and we think our suffering is endless, too. But each day does end and a new day does begin, and with it begins new hope and new possibilities.

Take this new day that you have been given and recognize it for what it is: a new chance.

Cherish each new day—for the new chance it represents, for the new passions you might feel.

Personal Power

*The thing women have got to learn is that nobody
gives you power. You just take it.*

ROSEANNE BARR

As females, we have watched all our lives while others had
the power—the power to rule, to dominate, and to abuse.
First it was our parents, then it was the men in our lives who
seemed to have all the power while we sat by and watched
them rule. If we were very, very good, sometimes those in
power would bestow on us some privilege or other, giving us
the feeling of having a little power ourselves, at least temporarily.

But now all that has changed. We can no longer afford to
stand idly by waiting for someone to throw us a crumb of
acknowledgment or power. Like Roseanne said, we have to
learn to take our power instead of expecting someone to give
it to us.

**Any power that is handed to you is probably not worth
having. Take your power.**

Fear of Your Power

Power can be seen as power with rather than power over,
and it can be used for competence and co-operation,
rather than dominance and control.

ANNE L. BARSTOW

It is a wonderful thing to finally get in touch with one's personal power—to feel the incredible intensity of it, to acknowledge the potential within us all. Unfortunately, most of us become afraid when we first glimpse our power and the potential for both good and evil it encompasses. In fact, most of us become so afraid of our power that we bury it so that we won't have to deal with it again for a long time.

Reclaim your personal power. Start gradually by standing up for what you want and what you believe in. Learn that you don't have to control anyone but yourself to have control over your own life.

Our personal power does indeed need to be respected, but it need not be buried in order for us to contain it and use it for good. Start uncovering your power a shovelful at a time, then take time to get used to it before you dig any deeper.

I will begin to own my personal power, learn to honor it, and use it for good.

Living Life to Its Fullest

*I don't want to get to the end of my life
and find that I have lived just the length of it.
I want to have lived the width of it as well.*

DIANE ACKERMAN

What does it mean to live a full life? It means not being afraid to let go of the old and to try something new. It means being willing to start all over again no matter how bad things get. It means being open to new experiences, new people, and new ideas. And most important, it means being able to look at yourself honestly, to learn and grow from your past mistakes, and continue trying to be the best you can be.

It isn't as important to live a long life as it is to live a full one.

Independence

No bird soars too high, if he soars with his own wings.

WILLIAM BLAKE

All your life people may have tried to convince you that you couldn't make it on your own. Your parents may have used your dependence on them as a way of controlling you. Your lovers and friends may have continually tried to make you doubt yourself and believe you couldn't live without them. In reality, they were afraid that if they didn't keep you down you would fly away and leave *them* alone.

Well, now you are ready to fly away. As time goes on, you will come to realize that there is no one holding you down any longer and you will be able to fly as high as you wish.

When we use our own wings there is no limit to how high we can fly.

The Road to Recovery

∽

Does the road wind uphill all the way?
Yes, to the very end.
Will the day's journey take the whole long day?
From morn to night, my friend.

CHRISTINA GEORGINA ROSSETTI
Uphill

The road to recovery is indeed uphill. Sometimes it will seem as if the journey will never end, that there is always something new to work on, always some new awareness that creates anxiety in you.

The fact is, the recovery journey never really ends. It will take a lifetime and then some. But as many philosophers have said, it's not the destination that matters, it's the journey itself. Learn to savor the journey. Stop along the way and appreciate your progress. Give yourself credit for how far you've come. Stop to smell the roses or better yet, to take a swim in the stream. Then, when you're ready, resume your journey, knowing full well that there really is no ending to it—that it is the journey that gives you strength.

If you focus only on reaching your destination, you will miss out on all the things you can learn along the way.

Regression

The human mind always makes progress,
but it is a progress in spirals.

MADAME DE STAËL

Most significant changes have no true beginning, middle, or end. Instead there is a continual progression toward a goal—a progression that sometimes falters, even halts altogether at times. There will be times when you feel you have gone backward instead of forward. But even at these times, be aware that you have regressed for a reason. For example, perhaps you needed to go back one more time to an abusive person, just to remind yourself how bad it feels to be negated, criticized, controlled, put down, or taken for granted.

When viewed in this light, regression can be seen as an inevitable, even positive, aspect of change. Whatever you do, do not be critical of yourself for having to learn a lesson one more time.

Often, the lessons we have learned the hard way are the ones that stick with us the longest.

Uncertainty

∾

The only thing that makes life possible is permanent,
intolerable uncertainty; not knowing what comes next.

URSULA K. LeGUIN

As frightening as uncertainty can be, it is what makes life interesting. If we could successfully predict what was going to happen tomorrow or the next day, it would take some of the adventure out of life. And if things always remained the same, if there were no surprises along the way, wouldn't life be boring? As frightening as uncertainty can be, it can be equally exciting.

Instead of fearing uncertainty, savor its excitement.

Heroine of Your Own Story

∞

We all live in suspense,
from day to day.
from hour to hour,
in other words,
we are the hero
of our own story.

MARY McCARTHY

There are no guarantees in life. None of us knows what will come tomorrow or the day after. No matter how much we plan, no matter how much we worry, things outside our control will happen. This can be terribly frightening for some people, but for others it can be exciting.

Sometimes, when I can stop planning and worrying, life suddenly becomes an adventure and I am the heroine. I wonder what kind of people I will be meeting in the future, what changes I will go through, and what new adventures lie ahead. You can do the same.

Begin to see your life as an adventure and find out how it feels to be the heroine of your own story.

The Spirit Within

It isn't until you come to a spiritual understanding of who
you are—not necessarily a religious feeling, but deep down,
the spirit within—that you can begin to take control.

OPRAH WINFREY

We are all physical, emotional, intellectual, and spiritual
beings, and coming to terms with the spiritual aspect of our
lives can be an important aspect of recovery. What exactly is
spirituality? Our spirituality consists of our belief in something beyond the tangible, fact-based reality of life, whether
it be a higher power, God, "the gods" or "goddesses," or our
own soul. Our spirituality can help us soar to the greatest
heights or delve into the deepest depths of our soul.

It is only by connecting with our spirit that we can completely know ourselves and thus have true control over our
own lives and our own destiny.

**The only person you need to control is yourself, and self-
control comes from knowing who you really are deep
inside.**

Celebrating Life

I like living. I have sometimes been wildly, despairingly,
acutely miserable, racked with sorrow, but through it all
I still know quite certainly that just to
be alive is a grand thing.

AGATHA CHRISTIE

Those of us who have suffered emotional and other kinds of
abuse sometimes lose track of how precious life is. The emotional abuse we have suffered can make us feel depressed and
hopeless to the point of wanting to give up or even to take
our own life.

Ironically, it sometimes takes a crisis, a failure, or even a
tragedy for us to begin to genuinely value our life. The
longer we are free from those who have emotionally torn us
down, the more chance we will have to begin to rebuild our
life, to raise our self-esteem and our spirits to the point
where we can begin to celebrate the life we were given.

**Celebrate your courage; celebrate your victories both large
and small; celebrate your freedom—celebrate your life!**

The Future

When I look into the future, it's so bright it burns my eyes.

OPRAH WINFREY

How I envy someone who can see the future in such a light. Most of us view the future through fearful eyes and see only the imagined darkness ahead. But for someone like Oprah, whose present life we can only imagine to be fulfilling and bright, the future would seem to hold more of the same. As your present life becomes more manageable and as you begin to accomplish some of the goals you have set for yourself, your future will begin to look brighter, too.

We envision our future based not only on our past but also our present.

Inner Peace

There is no way to peace. Peace is the way.

A. J. MUSTE

What a wonderful feeling to experience inner peace—to feel the quiet calm of self-satisfaction instead of the constant churning of self-doubt and self-criticism; to be able to relax into oneself, to float with oneself instead of always paddling upstream.

As hard as it may be for you to believe, you too can gain inner peace. No one ever experiences inner peace at all times, and we have to pay attention to ourselves in order to realize that we are feeling inner peace.

Ironically, this is what happened to me recently while on a plane trip. I was working on this very entry and looking out the window at the clouds below when I suddenly realized, much to my surprise, that I was indeed feeling very peaceful inside, more peaceful than I probably have ever felt. Had I not been writing about inner peace, I wouldn't have even noticed it.

Inner peace comes with self-acceptance, self-assuredness, maturity, and learning to let go—of expectations, shoulds, and things having to be a certain way.

Your Journey

*I think that wherever your journey takes you,
there are new gods waiting there, with divine patience—
and laughter.*

SUSAN M. WATKINS

What a wonderful image—the gods waiting for us along our path, guiding us with a patient spirit and a sense of humor.

Whether you believe in God, in "the gods," in guardian angels, or in your own higher self, there truly is a higher power that guides you and looks after you. Wherever you go and whatever you do, this higher power is there for you if you tap into it and listen to its voice. Your higher power will tell you which direction to take when you reach a crossroads, when to stop along the way to rest, and when to begin your journey again.

Wherever your journey takes you, keep your eyes open for new gods.

The Source of Happiness

It is not easy to find happiness in ourselves,
and it is impossible to find it elsewhere.

AGNES REPPLIER

We must look within ourselves for happiness instead of look-ing to someone else to provide it for us. Any happiness we find with others is only temporary unless we come to terms with who we are. The true source of happiness is to know ourselves, accept ourselves, and thus find peace with our-selves.

I am the source of my own happiness.

Finding Your Own Light

I will work in my own way,
according to the light that is in me.

LYDIA MARIA CHILD

We must each be true to ourselves and work in our own unique way instead of trying to mold ourselves into someone we aren't or to do things the way others would do them. We each have our own light within us—meaning we have our own unique purpose in life, our own path to find.

When we are true to ourselves and follow our own path, we find that our light truly does shine.

Meeting the Challenge

*We never know how high we are
Till we are called to rise
And then if we are true to plan
Our statures touch the skies.*

EMILY DICKINSON

It is through our struggles that we discover how strong we are. It isn't until we are challenged to do things that we feel are beyond our abilities that we discover we can accomplish more than we thought possible. Starting a new life after ending a relationship or a job may seem impossible, especially when you feel so damaged by the emotional abuse, but you are capable of it. You will discover your true mettle once you meet the challenge.

You can meet the challenge—whatever it is.

Happy Endings

*All the powers work so that you should come to a bad
ending, but our soul works for the opposite—that the ending
should be good. Actually, the ending is always good.*

ISAAC BASHEVIS SINGER

Whether we recognize it or not, every ending is good. It is
good because of what we have learned along the way. It is
good because with each ending is a new beginning. It is good
because it is as it should be.

Every ending is a happy ending.

Dreams

Reach high, for stars lie hidden in your soul. Dream deep,
for every dream precedes the goal.

PAMELA VAULL STARR

We must allow ourselves to dream and to reach for the stars,
for it is only by dreaming that we can discover our true
potential. Those who don't allow themselves to dream are so
earthbound that they can't touch the stars. Dreamers, on the
other hand, are the movers and shakers, the pioneers, the
cosmic explorers.

So dream high and dream deep. Dream of things you
want to do, the kind of person you want to be, the kind of
world you'd like to live in. Dream on, because dreams can
change reality.

If anyone accuses you of being a dreamer—thank him.

About the Author

Beverly Engel, M.F.C.C., has spent 17 years helping people in abusive and dysfunctional relationships both as a therapist and a bestselling author. *The Right to Innocence, Divorcing a Parent, The Emotionally Abused Woman,* and *Partners in Recovery* are all recognized as leading books in the area of abuse. She has shared her expertise on "Oprah!," "Donahue," and "Sally Jesse Raphael." She is the founder and director of the Center for Adult Survivors of Sexual Abuse (CASSA) and currently maintains a private practice in Southern California.